The Mirror
of God's Word

A Biblical View of Physical Beauty

"As for me, I will behold thy face in righteousness: I shall be satisfied, when I awake, with thy likeness" (Ps. 17:15).

The Mirror of God's Word

A Biblical View of Physical Beauty

By

Robin Parton

The Mirror of God's Word; A Biblical View of Physical Beauty
© 2020 by Robin Parton

ISBN: 978-1-63073-343-8
eBook ISBN: 978-1-63073-345-2

Front cover picture by Amber Andrews of
Amber Andrews Photography

Scripture was taken from the Authorized King James Version.

Published in the United States of America by Faithful Life Publishers, North Fort Myers, FL 33903

FaithfulLifePublishers.com
info@flpublishers.com

888.720.0950

24 23 22 21 20   1 2 3 4 5

Dedication

This book is dedicated to the ladies in our family. It is my desire as your mom, mother-in-law, and Nanny to give you a biblical view regarding your physical beauty. This manuscript was prepared first and foremost for you, Cyndi, Lydia, Julia, Ruth, Allie, Aleah, Anne, Lana, Violet, Aubree, and any other ladies God may send to our family. I love each of you so very much!

Table of Contents

Foreword

by Dan Parton

Although no author has been officially ascribed to it, this late 19th century American nursery rhyme, *Star Light, Star Bright*, has been a part of our memory for most all our lives:

> *Star light, star bright,*
>
> *The first star I see tonight;*
>
> *I wish I may, I wish I might,*
>
> *Have the wish I wish tonight.*

The theme of wishing upon a star has been expressed in many tales. This particular nursery rhyme has been used time and again when putting a child to bed. We can just imagine a child gazing wishfully out her window up into a star-studded sky hoping her every wish will come true. After all, every child has a wish for something. It is always for something she does not have, something better.

Though we eventually outgrow the nursery rhyme stage, we do not always outgrow the making of a "wish for something better" stage. As adults, we still toss coins into wishing wells or fountains fantasizing that our adult wishes will somehow come true.

Every young girl's wish is to grow up pretty and perhaps someday become someone's beautiful princess. We've all seen the young girls in fairy tales who become beautiful princesses destined to be married to a handsome prince. However, it doesn't always work out that way. In fact, it most always does not work out the way her wish was imagined.

The book you are about to read, personally, practically, compassionately and biblically addresses the issue of beauty from a vantage point few have even attempted to address. Chapter by chapter, you will learn how our loving God speaks concerning this all-too-often misunderstood subject. You will learn how important it is to learn God's viewpoint on the matter and just how important it is that we know and understand His perfect wisdom.

This book has been lovingly and painfully pressed from the author's heart. Robin's personal experience and dedication to accurate biblical interpretation has been the foundational undergirding for all she has written herein. In other words, she's been there and done that. This makes the truths she shares in each chapter more credible than had it been written from one who has never been there or ever done that. Her appearance was changed after her operation. No one can honestly deny that, even though some have attempted to convince her otherwise. However, let me say that she is as pretty as she has always been, and the lessons she has learned have caused her to glow even more beautifully!

This honest and revealing book leaves no stone unturned. Every girl who takes the time to read this book, will not just learn, but will also be challenged to become all that God desires her to become. Truly the words of John 8:32 will take on new meaning for any girl wanting to be set free from the personal and societal pressures placed upon her to find her value in her physical appearance, "And ye shall know the truth, and the truth shall make you free."

Preface

Mother's Day, 2018 was a month before our 40th wedding anniversary which was just a few days before I was scheduled to have major surgery to remove a brain tumor. Although I did not enjoy reading through all of the possible complications of this surgery, I was thankful for the opportunity to prepare. I knew

there was a slight possibility of losing my facial nerves which could permanently alter my physical appearance. In light of this possibility, I wanted our children to have one last photograph of my pre-surgical appearance, so my husband and I drove to one of my favorite photo spots to get this shot.

My surgery took place in a teaching hospital, so there were many doctors involved. All of them, with the exception of my surgeon, believed my facial paralysis was permanent. From the very first glance at my post-surgical appearance, I recognized my need for God's grace. I have experienced enough in my life to know I would receive that grace as I humbled myself before my loving Heavenly Father and sought His comfort from the Word of God. This picture was taken with our daughter, one week after surgery on our first outing to my eye doctor.

Video chatting with our children and grandchildren after surgery was difficult for me. Our oldest son, Jon, has remained very complimentary and positive during my time of adjusting to new limitations and a new physical appearance.

Our youngest son, Jack, challenged me when he said, "Mom, whether God heals your face or not, we know you will use this to bring glory to God." Nine months after surgery I sought to do just that when I wrote my first Bible study on a biblical view of physical beauty. It was then I realized I had only scratched the surface of this important subject.

When I mentioned the possibility of writing a book on this subject to our son, Dave, he asked me, "Mom, what if your book is never published? Is it enough for you to simply preserve what God is teaching you for the girls in our family?" Yes, Dave, and here it is.

Acknowledgments

First and foremost, I am thankful for my husband, who planted the desire within my heart to not only read the Word of God, but also to study it. Many years ago, he gifted me with my first three study books: *The Interlinear Greek-English New Testament*, *Vine's Expository Dictionary of Old and New Testament Words*, and *Wilson's Old Testament Word Studies*. All of the definitions in this book come from these sources, unless otherwise stated. I can still remember the very first time I looked up a word in the Bible, and the thrill it gave me to have further insight into what God was teaching in the passage. I have never tired of gaining a clearer understanding of our God and His Word.

I am so thankful for those who have given hours of their time so that I would have additional study materials to consult in preparing this manuscript such as my *Liberty Bible Commentary*, *Matthew Henry Commentary*, *All the Women of the Bible* by Herbert Lockyer, and *Rose Book of Bible Charts, Maps & Time Lines*.

I am also thankful for the various biblical counseling ministries God has used in my life to transform me from being an insecure woman, who hid behind her husband, to one who is now willing to obey the commandment found in Titus 2:4-5 to, *"…teach the young women to be sober, to love their husbands, to love their children, To be discreet, chaste, keepers at home, good, obedient to their own husbands, that the word of God be not blasphemed."* I currently hold certifications from Women Counseling Women, taught by Mrs. Debi Pryde, and Hope Biblical Counseling Center, founded and directed by Dr. Terry L. Coomer.

Of course, I could not have done this without the aid of my three editors. Each of them has differing levels of education, yet they have chosen to serve the Lord by helping me prepare a manuscript that would bring honor and glory to God. Does this mean my book is flawless? I doubt it, but I have a dedicated group of ladies, who have given hours of their time, to do their best to help me produce a manuscript free from mistakes that would distract from the truths of God's Word. Thank you Lois Moyer, Tracey Craft, and Sandy Rempel for laboring together with me for the cause of Christ.

I am also thankful for the ministry of Faithful Life Publishers. I am so very grateful for the way in which God directed me to this ministry. It is refreshing to do business with folks who are ministry minded.

Lastly, I want to thank all of those who encouraged me to preserve my experience in book form, and specifically those who encouraged me to write in a Bible study format. God used you to help me take the first step toward completing this manuscript.

There is no person, ministry, or study book that can do what the Word of God can do in our hearts. One of my favorite verses is found in Ephesians 3:20: *"Now unto him that is able to do exceeding abundantly above all that we ask or think, according to the power that worketh in us."* I want to praise the Living Word for giving us the written Word, *"…for it is the power of God unto salvation to every one that believeth; to the Jew first, and also to the Greek. For therein is the righteousness of God revealed from faith to faith: as it is written, The just shall live by faith"* (Rom. 1:16-17). All scripture is quoted from the Authorized King James Version.

Introduction

When I began this project, I truly did not know if I would be able to find enough material for an entire six-week study on the subject of physical beauty. I began with the Bible study I completed after my surgery and divided it up into various subjects for more in-depth research. I had a general idea of the material I wanted to cover and asked the Lord for His direction as I began the study for each week. I could clearly see His hand as He provided the substance through many different avenues. There were times when something was said in a sermon that prompted the next idea and times when God would bring to mind one principle while I was studying another. There were also times when I spent hours studying a principle and then chose not to use it because in the end it was not applicable, or really did not add anything to what God had already made very clear.

As I approached this subject, I knew in my heart I would need these truths first and foremost; however, I did not realize until the last few months how the Lord would use them to prepare my heart to accept the permanent changes He has allowed in my appearance. Over and over again, He has shown me where my focus needs to be. He has revealed to me those areas that He considers to be beautiful, and those attributes He desires for me to possess. During these months of looking into the mirror of God's Word, He has brought me to a place of contentment.

I have been in full-time ministry with my husband for over 40 years. As I was maturing in age, and the problems of women were intensifying, I felt the need for further training. For the last several years, I have sought that training through various biblical counseling courses. While this book is broken up into a six-week Bible study, I have been studying the truths contained herein for years. I have been recording these truths along with their application to physical beauty now for over 18 months. Please do not become overwhelmed if you do not comprehend these truths in a six-week time frame because I certainly did not. This is an intense study, so you may need to extend it beyond six weeks. Take the time you need to study the scripture texts and apply them to your individual situation. If you choose to use this resource in a Sunday school class or ladies' Bible study, I believe you and your ladies will find working on the assignments together very enjoyable.

It has simply been my desire to share the principles the Lord has taught me and used to shape my biblical view of physical beauty. May you, too, learn and grow and come to a place of total surrender and contentment as you join me in looking into the mirror of God's Word.

Week One

Mirror, Mirror on the Wall

Something to Think About

The original phrase, "Mirror, mirror, on the wall, who in this land is fairest of all?" came from the German fairy tale, *Snow White*, by the Brothers Grimm. Walt Disney Productions produced *Snow White and the Seven Dwarfs* as the first full-length animated movie in 1937. Many of us have seen, or have read the story of Snow White's evil stepmother gazing into her magic mirror to find out who was the fairest in all the land. More than 80 years later, we find women are still gazing into mirrors and asking this same question. Who is the fairest, the prettiest, the most beautiful? Is this even a question Christian women should entertain? Many of the princess stories with which we grew up do emphasize the good character qualities in the princesses such as their work ethic, their kindness, and truthfulness; however, I fear our young girls primarily pick up on their beauty. It would be so much easier to focus on the character qualities of the princesses if they were average looking women with an average build dressed in simple, modest clothing.

Needless to say, by a very young age, we form an opinion about what we see when we look into a mirror. If we have not been taught a biblical view of beauty, that opinion is often based upon what others say about us and about how we are treated in relation to our appearance. As a child in elementary school, I can remember being in a Halloween parade. My sister had beautiful, long, blonde hair that hung in ringlets, so naturally she was chosen by my mother to play the part of Goldilocks and ride in a wagon pulled by my younger sister, my brother, and me. My younger sister and I had short brown hair, so it only made sense that we would play the parts of Mama Bear and Baby Bear, while my brother played the part of Papa Bear. We covered our faces with bear masks and wore costumes that were so large they fit over our coats allowing us to at least be warm. Sadly, I remember being very jealous of my middle sister and wishing I could be the beautiful Goldilocks riding in the wagon.

The fifth grade was a defining year for me as I began to feel the sting of the opinions of others. I was one in a group of five girls who hung out together. One of the boys in our class came to visit us at one of our "club meetings" and during that visit, he made the comment that I was just too ugly to kiss. Then during choir tryouts, I was the only girl asked to sit down along with several boys. When it came time for our group to pantomime a song by a popular quartet, it was decided that I should run the record player since only four singers were needed and everyone already knew I could not sing. I did not sing for three years after that. It took me learning how to play the alto notes of some of the more familiar hymns on the piano until I had them memorized to finally open my mouth and sing again.

I grew up in inner-city Harrisburg, Pennsylvania. My parents became concerned about some of the things that were happening in the inner-city schools, so, the following year, they placed us in a Christian school. One would think Christian school students would be kinder than those attending the public schools, but immediately I was teased about my glasses. I was a pretty fast runner on the track team, but it did not take long for the boys to begin to call me the girl with the bird name and the elephant legs. Then in high school one of the boys decided my nose was too big. Anytime I would turn around to talk to one of my girlfriends the boys would hold their arms up to guard themselves while saying, "Look out Dukes (my maiden name) you almost hit me with your nose." They even went so far as to draw my profile on the chalk board extending my nose around the room on the paneled walls. During my junior high and some of my high school years our church participated in the area Youth for Christ skating parties once a month. I loved skating to the organ music, but I hated being one of the girls left standing at the end of the rink when the boys would skate around and choose a partner. When I finally did get a real boyfriend, he did not tell me I was pretty, but rather that I did the best with what I had. This is not exactly what every girl wants to hear.

Since I was reared by a father who loved to tease, I was able to laugh at most of these insults, but inside I was forming an opinion about what I saw when I looked into the mirror. Thankfully, my father knew my struggles with wearing glasses and allowed me to get contact lenses during my senior year of high school. He also offered to take me to a cosmetic specialist where I could learn to apply make-up properly, but I did not even want to be around women who specialized in beauty products. I cannot speak for others who have struggled with a proper view of how God created them, but I felt if I could simply achieve in some other area of my life, I could compensate for what I perceived as my lack of physical beauty. I was good in academics, pretty decent in athletics, and fair in artistic abilities, but I did not excel in any of those. As I have grown in my walk with God, I no longer believe God wants us to make up for what we feel is an undesirable appearance by excelling in some other area of life. I believe He wants us to have a biblical view of how He created us and of what true beauty is. I had not thought much about this in relation to the Word of God until I came out of surgery to remove a benign brain tumor which caused drastic changes to my appearance.

On May 1, 2018, I was diagnosed with a fast-growing acoustic tumor, and surgery to have it removed was set for June 14. There was a long list of possible complications with varying percentages of probability. Among them were the following: A 30% chance I would lose all of my hearing in my right ear, and I did; a less than 5% chance I would awaken with facial paralysis, but I did. Because the chances of facial paralysis were so slim, I did not even notice it could cause dryness to my cornea due to not being able to close my eye. The area of greatest pain came from the eye disorder I developed as a result of my dry cornea, and the only way it would heal was to apply ointment to my eye several times each day. It took over nine months until I could begin to drive again locally due to the distortion caused by the ointment. Of course, this also meant I would once again have to resort to wearing glasses since my eye was too damaged to use my contact lenses.

My daughter came out to Colorado to help care for me, and the following is an update she posted just three days after surgery:

She had another good night. Her occupational therapist was in this morning and made the comment that she is physically strong. Her core is strong, her legs are strong, and this will really be very helpful in her recovery. She helped mom practice getting in and out of the shower as well as sitting down and standing up. With the depth perception, she explained that one of the challenges will be that she will not be able to tell where a stair ends and the next one begins, so we will need to put yellow tape on the edge of the stairs at home. Granted, she won't be taking any stairs any time soon. The doctor explains more to us each day. Today, he explained that her right vestibular, or balance nerve, is dead. It was preserved during surgery, but it is now dead. Eventually her left balance nerve will compensate for the right one that is dead. This will take time and physical therapy. It is neat to hear how our bodies naturally work things out. Her right hearing nerve is also dead. That is old news though, and it will be an adjustment. We will need to talk louder and try to talk to her on her left side. We were all laughing yesterday because both my dad and I wear hearing aids, and now mom is deaf on one side. There have been some communication issues to say the least.

Her right facial nerve is the one in question. The doctor said it could be annoyed, but he believes it is dead. As of this morning there is still no movement on the right side of her face all the way from the top of her forehead to the bottom of her chin. For instance, she cannot close her right eye, so for now until God heals her, she will do eye drops every hour, all day, every day, and at night, she will put ointment on and tape her eye shut. This will, hopefully, prevent any damage to her eye, but this is a big concern. She cannot blink; she cannot close it to sleep. She will need to learn to chew again and take a drink again. She does okay with a straw, but you can tell it is a big challenge for her; there are so many little things I would never have thought of.

We have lots of different things to pray for obviously, but today I'm asking you all to specifically pray for her spirit. Everything is sinking in this morning. She made the comment, "I was prepared to lose my hearing. I was prepared to have some balance issues, but I did not think I would look like this. I feel like I'm a freak." I tried to assure her that much of what she is seeing now is swelling from being pumped up with so many fluids, and her black eye/right cheek will go back to normal. However, things have changed and will be her new reality until God chooses to heal her. I assured her again that she is beautiful and that even if her smile has changed a little, I can still see Jesus shining through it and through her eyes. I have seen her tears today for the first time since surgery.

We are so thankful for all the progress she is making. We know that all her issues can be worked through, and we, of course, know that looks are not everything or even anything really. However, these things still affect us, and take time to process and accept. Please pray that God will comfort her as she goes through all the emotions. I was talking to my daughter, Allie, last night who is seven, and she asked about Nanny and said she wanted to FaceTime with her soon. I explained that Nanny is the same Nanny, but that she looks just a little different. She said, "Mom, I already know. Daddy showed me her picture. She is so pretty and all of her family, and friends, and God will still think she is beautiful too." I told that to mom, and she just cried. She said her heart needed that.

It would almost seem cruel that God would allow this in the life of someone who had already dealt with much teasing and criticism about her appearance, but we do not have a cruel God. It is totally against His character to inflict pain out of cruelty. As soon as I said "I feel like I'm a freak" the Holy Spirit of God convicted my heart that my thinking was wrong. I am not proud of this reaction to what I saw in the mirror that morning, and I knew right then and there that if I was going to be able to have a good spirit about the change in my appearance, it was important for me to spend as little time as possible in front of a mirror. I also knew that I needed to look into the mirror of God's Word to align my thoughts with His. Therefore, I invite you to join me as we look into God's Word to align our thoughts with His on this matter of physical beauty.

We do not find the word "mirror" in the Bible, but the word "glass" or "looking glass" is often interpreted as a mirror. The first example of a mirror goes as far back as Exodus 38:8: *"And he made the laver of brass, and the foot of it of brass, of the lookingglasses of the women assembling, which assembled at the door of the tabernacle of the congregation."* The Tabernacle was meticulously designed as a picture of Christ and His salvation. It sat toward the back of the courtyard and was divided into two sections that were separated by a curtain. The first section was the Holy Place and it contained three pieces of furniture each signifying a different aspect of our relationship to Christ. The Candlestick signified the understanding that Jesus gives to men, the Table of Shewbread signified the fellowship or communion we can have with Christ, and the Altar of Incense signified prayer. The priest would enter this first section each day to care for the various pieces of furniture; however, the second section was only entered once each year and only by the High Priest. It was called the Holy of Holies and contained the Ark of the Covenant which was covered with the Mercy Seat containing the golden Cherubims. It was here the High Priest would enter on the Day of Atonement and sprinkle the blood of the sacrificial lamb to atone for the sins of the nation.

The Laver of Brass, in the outer courtyard, was located between the entrance of the Tabernacle and the Altar of Burnt Offering, or the Brazen Altar. As the people entered the courtyard, they would come to the Brazen Altar where they would offer their sacrifice symbolizing there can be no forgiveness of sin without the shedding of blood. The priest would then wash both his hands and feet in the Laver of Brass before entering the Tabernacle. The Laver of Brass was made of bronze mirrors donated by the women who served at the Tabernacle, and it signified two important truths. The brass looking glasses symbolized the Bible revealing sin and the water in the Laver symbolized the cleansing of sin.

Read Hebrews Chapter 9, and answer the following question:

1. Who is our High Priest, and what did He offer for our redemption?

Read Mathew 27:45-51, and answer the following questions:

1. What happened in the temple when Jesus died on the cross?

2. Do you have any idea why this happened, or why it is significant?

Yesterday, we concluded our study with the veil of the temple being split from top to bottom when Jesus died on the cross. This symbolizes our access to God through the shed blood of Jesus Christ. We learned that the Laver of Brass (looking glasses) symbolized both the revealing of sin and the cleansing of sin. Today we will look at another illustration for the use of a mirror in Bible times.

A mirror is one of three illustrations God uses to show the purpose of His law. In James 1:23-25 we read: *"For if any be a hearer of the word, and not a doer, he is like unto a man beholding his natural face in a glass: For he beholdeth himself, and goeth his way, and straightway forgetteth what manner of man he was. But whoso looketh into the perfect law of liberty, and continueth therein, he being not a forgetful hearer, but a doer of the work, this man shall be blessed in his deed."* In this passage of Scripture, we see the example of a person looking into a mirror, but it is not simply to get a glance of himself. This is speaking of someone who would bend over for a close look, much like we would do if we noticed a blemish on our face and would move in closely to examine it further in order to deal with it.

1. When you look into a mirror and see something that needs attention, the mirror cannot correct the problem for you. Why then is the mirror necessary?

Not only is the Law of God compared to a mirror, but it is also compared to a plumb line in Amos 7:7-8: *"Thus he shewed me: and, behold, the Lord stood upon a wall made by a plumbline, with a plumbline in his hand. And the LORD said unto me, Amos, what seest thou? And I said, A plumbline. Then said the Lord, Behold, I will set a plumbline in the midst of my people Israel: I will not again pass by them any more."* A plumb line is a line with a plumb bob, or weight, at the end of it, and it is typically held next to a vertical line to show whether or not that vertical line is straight.

   2. Based upon this definition, can a plumb line fix the crooked surface it reveals?

In this particular passage, the plumb line is compared to the Law of God which showed the nation of Israel just how far they had wandered from God's standard.

We have yet a third illustration of the how the Law of God was used in Galatians 3:24-25: *"Wherefore the law was our schoolmaster to bring us unto Christ, that we might be justified by faith. But after that faith is come, we are no longer under a schoolmaster."* It is the schoolmaster that brings the student to the teacher. (The schoolmaster is not the teacher.)

By now you may be wondering what in the world this has to do with beauty. I simply ask you to bear with me as I lay some important ground-work for the weeks ahead.

On Day 2, we talked about the first mention of mirrors in the Bible, and we briefly explained the importance of the Tabernacle and the furniture it contained. Even with its importance in the Old Testament, the blood of bulls and goats did not save men and women. *"For it is not possible that the blood of bulls and of goats should take away sins"* (Heb. 10:4).

3. According to 1 Peter 1:18-21, we are redeemed by what?

So far, we have looked at a brief history of mirrors in the Bible. We have seen how they were used in the fashioning of the Laver of Brass. We have also seen how the law of God was compared to a mirror by revealing our sin and our need of a Saviour. Please allow me to take these Old Testament illustrations and apply them to our lives. We have all found the use of mirrors to be helpful in revealing areas of our physical appearance that may be in need of correction. If we do not see a problem, we will not realize the need to correct the problem. Sin, in each of our lives, causes a great problem for us. In Isaiah 59:2 we read the following: *"But your iniquities have separated between you and your God, and your sins have hid his face from you, that he will not hear."* Not only does sin cause us a problem in this life, but it causes us to be separated from God for all eternity.

Thankfully, God has provided a way for correcting this problem; it is called reconciliation. To be reconciled means "to be changed from one condition to another, so as to remove all enmity and leave no impediment to unity and peace." In Colossians 1:20-21 we read the following: *"And, having made peace through the blood of his cross, by him to reconcile all things unto himself; by him, I say, whether they be things in earth, or things in heaven. And you, that were sometime alienated and enemies in your mind by wicked works, yet now hath he reconciled."* How, then, can one be reconciled to God?

1. First, we must acknowledge that we are sinners. The mirror of God's Word clearly reveals this to us in Romans 3:23 says: *"For all have sinned, and come short of the glory of God."* That word "all" is inclusive. No one is exempt. We are all born sinners. Romans 5:12 says: *"Wherefore, as by one man sin entered into the world, and death by sin; and so death passed upon all men,*

for that all have sinned." A sin is any time we disobey God and go against His laws.

2. Because we are sinners, we do not deserve to go to Heaven; we deserve to go to Hell. As Romans 5:12 states, not only was sin passed on to us from Adam but so was death. God looks at death differently than we do. The Bible explains after our physical death, we deserve a "second death," which is separation from God forever in Hell. Revelation 21:8 explains: *"But the fearful, and unbelieving, and the abominable, and murderers, and whoremongers, and sorcerers, and idolaters, and all liars, shall have their part in the lake which burneth with fire and brimstone: which is the second death."* This is hard to accept, but I must be truthful with you. I am no better than you, and you are no better than I am. I am a sinner, and you are a sinner. I deserve to go to Hell, and so do you. If this were all there was to it, we would surely have no hope; but the Bible goes on to give us a remedy for our dire situation.

3. Jesus paid for our sins when He shed His blood and died on the cross then rose again the third day. Romans 6:23 says: *"For the wages of sin is death; but the gift of God is eternal life through Jesus Christ our Lord."* Eternal life is a gift. You can do nothing to earn it. Galatians 2:16 states: *"Knowing that a man is not justified* (declared righteous) *by the works of the law, but by the faith of Jesus Christ, even we have believed in Jesus Christ, that we might be justified by the faith of Christ, and not by the works of the law: for by the works of the law shall no flesh be justified."* Just like a gift is purchased for you, eternal life was purchased for you by Jesus' sacrifice on the cross. Romans 5:8-10 says: *"But God commendeth* (proved) *his love toward us, in that, while we were yet sinners, Christ died for us. Much more then, being now justified by his blood, we shall be saved from wrath through him.*

For if, when we were enemies, we were reconciled to God by the death of his Son, much more, being reconciled, we shall be saved by his life." Since we are all sinners, we need Someone perfect to take our place. Jesus did that by dying on the cross for us, but He did not stay dead. He arose from the grave! Romans 6:9 states: *"Knowing that Christ being raised from the dead dieth no more; death hath no more dominion* (power) *over him."* Jesus is able to give us eternal life because He conquered death. The grave had no power over Him!

4. There is only one way to be reconciled to God and receive His gift of eternal life. Romans 10:13 says: *"For whosoever shall call upon the name of the Lord shall be saved."* That word "whosoever" is another inclusive word. It means anyone. In context, the word "call" does not mean to call on God to help you out of a hard circumstance; it means to call to place your trust in Jesus to save you from your sin. Jesus did everything so that we might be reconciled to God. He suffered, bled, and died for each one of us.

Have you accepted God's gift of salvation and placed your trust in Jesus alone to save you from your sin? If you have not and would like to place your trust in Him, just pray to Him and tell Him. Here is an example of what to say, but these are not "magic words;" they are simply an example. You must mean them from your heart. "Dear Jesus, I know I am a sinner. I know I deserve to be separated from you forever in Hell. Thank you for dying on the cross for me. I place my trust in you, Jesus, and only You to save me and take me to Heaven when I die. Thank you for saving me. Amen."

If you have prayed this prayer or something similar to it, I have wonderful news for you. In John 1:12 we read the following: *"But as many as received him, to them gave he power to become the sons of God, even to them that believe on his name."* According to this verse it is our responsibility to simply believe and receive, or accept, Jesus Christ as our Saviour. It is God's responsibility to honor His promise to give us the authority to become children of God.

When we go through difficulties in life, particularly ones of a very personal nature, it is important to have a support system in place. There is no greater support one can receive than from God the Father, God the Son, and God the Holy Spirit. No matter how thoroughly one will try to explain the emotions they are experiencing to those around them, the explanation will often be met with misunderstanding or an attempt to sugar-coat the trial. No one understands the human heart better than our Heavenly Father.

I want to challenge you to take a few minutes today and write out your salvation testimony. If you use a journal, you may want to write it there, or you may want to write it in the back of this book, but write it down somewhere. Knowing we have access to God through the shed blood of Jesus Christ is foundational to any Bible study, but especially to one so personally directed to the way in which He chose to create us. Once you have written out your salvation testimony, take a few minutes to meditate on what this means to you and thank Him for His sacrifice for you.

Over the last three days, we have looked at the illustration of a mirror being likened to the Laver of Brass which showed us our need of cleansing, and the law of God which revealed to us our need of a Saviour. Then you allowed me to take a few minutes and share with you the gospel of Jesus Christ. Now I must ask, have you been saved? Have you accepted God's gift of eternal life purchased for you by His Son, Jesus, when He died in your place on the cross? If you still struggle with being able to answer these questions, then I would challenge you to talk to someone, perhaps the person who gave this book to you.

Galatians 3:26 says, *"For ye are all the children of God by faith in Christ Jesus."* If you have settled this matter and know beyond a shadow of doubt that you are a child of God through faith in Jesus, then I would like to take some time today to look at just some of the things that happen in our lives when we get saved. In Romans 8:1-4 we read: *"There is therefore now no condemnation to them which are in Christ Jesus, who walk not after the flesh, but after the Spirit. For the law of the Spirit of life in Christ Jesus hath made me free from the law of sin and death. For what the law could not do, in that it was weak through the flesh, God sending his own Son in the likeness of sinful flesh, and for sin, condemned sin in the flesh: That the righteousness of the law might be fulfilled in us, who walk not after the flesh, but after the Spirit."* Is this not exciting!

Once we are saved, we no longer need to fear death and an eternity separated from God in Hell, but that is just the beginning of the blessings we gain when we place our trust in Jesus Christ.

1. According to Hebrews 4:16, what is one privilege of being a child of God?

2. According to Hebrews 13:5, what comfort do we have as a child of God?

3. According to John 10:11, 27-29, Jesus is our what?

4. According to the previous passage of Scripture, in whose hands are we held?

When we get saved not only do we become a part of God's family with all of the privileges that come with having a Heavenly Father, not only do we find in Jesus a caring gentle Shepherd, but we also have a constant companion in the Holy Spirit, our Comforter. The word "Comforter" means "one who is called along-side to help." Jesus promised His disciples He would send another Comforter when He left them to go to His Heavenly Father. This Comforter would be just like Jesus, and He would continue to provide the strength Jesus had provided for them.

5. Read John 14:16-18, 26; Romans 8:10-16, and list the things the Holy Spirit does for us.

There is simply no way we could cover all that becomes available to us at the moment of our salvation, but part of the excitement of the Christian life is growing in our knowledge of God. *"Grace and peace be multiplied unto you through the knowledge of God, and of Jesus our Lord, According as his divine power hath given unto us all things that pertain unto life and godliness, through the knowledge of him that hath called us to glory and virtue"* (2 Peter 1:2-3). Just as we gain more appreciation for our earthly fathers and mothers as we learn more about them and the lives they lived before we entered, we gain more appreciation for all we have in our God as we study the Word of God. Our earthy parents may, or may not, have been good examples of our Heavenly Father. In either case, growing in our knowledge of God brings both the grace and the peace we need as we look closely into the mirror of God's Word to gain the contentment we need to live with the circumstances He has allowed.

Today, we are going to look at yet another use for the word "mirror" found in 2 Corinthians 3:17 and 18: *"Now the Lord is that Spirit: and where the Spirit of the Lord is, there is liberty. But we all, with open face beholding as in a glass* (mirror) *the glory of the Lord, are changed into the same image from glory to glory, even as by the Spirit of the Lord."* Prior to salvation we were in bondage to sin and its consequences, as found in Romans 8:2: *"For the law of the Spirit of life in Christ Jesus hath made me free from the law of sin and death,"* and Romans 6:23a: *"For the wages of sin is death..."* We may have been trying to save ourselves by seeking to obey the laws of God, but once we reject this thinking and believe on the Lord Jesus Christ for our salvation, the Bible says there is liberty. There is liberty in our access to God and a freedom from the bondage to sin.

There are several schools of thought on the meaning of verse eighteen. Some believe the word "mirror" found in 2 Corinthians 3:18 is referring again to the Word of God; some believe it refers to Christ; and yet others believe it refers to the believer's heart. I would like to submit another thought based upon both my *Liberty Bible Commentary* and *Matthew Henry Commentary* that this is actually referring to the believer himself reflecting the glory of the Lord. I am not a Bible scholar, but I do know that it is God's will for us to be conformed to His Image, and therefore I submit the following scriptures to you for further study:

- *"For whom he did foreknow, he also did predestinate to be conformed to the image of his Son, that he might be the firstborn among many brethren"* (Rom. 8:29).

- *"And as we have borne the image of the earthy, we shall also bear the image of the heavenly"* (1 Cor. 15:49).

- *"My little children, of whom I travail in birth again until Christ be formed in you"* (Gal. 4:19).

Have you ever met someone who seemed to just radiate the glory of the Lord? I have, although I do not want that experience to dictate my belief. When I read the story of Moses on the mount, I am fascinated by the fact that spending time in the presence of the Lord actually affected his appearance: *"And it came to pass, when Moses came down from mount Sinai with the two tables of testimony in Moses' hand, when he came down from the mount, that Moses wist not that the skin of his face shone while he talked with him"* (Ex. 34:29). Moses did not realize what had happened to his appearance; it was simply a byproduct of spending time in the presence of the Lord.

My love for this story may be one of the reasons why one of my favorite readings is the *Refiner of Silver*. The author of the *Refiner of Silver* is unknown, but I sure would love to be able to thank him or her for such a clear picture of how God refines our lives. Once you have read it, answer the question below.

Refiner of Silver

Some time ago, a few ladies met to read the Scriptures. While reading the third chapter of Malachi, they came upon a remarkable expression in the third verse, *"And He shall sit as a refiner and purifier of silver."*

One lady's opinion was that it was intended to convey the view of the sanctifying influence of the grace of Christ. Then, she proposed to visit a silversmith and would report to her friends what he said on the subject. She went; and without telling the objective of her errand, begged to know the process of refining silver, which he fully described to her.

"But, Sir," she said, "do you sit while the work of refining is going on?" "Oh, yes, Madam," replied the silversmith, "I must sit with my eye steadily fixed on the furnace; for if the time necessary for refining is exceeded in the slightest degree, the silver will be injured." The lady at once saw the beauty and comfort too of the expression, *He shall sit as a refiner and purifier of silver.* Christ sees it needful to put His children into a furnace. His eye is steadily intent on the work of purifying, and His wisdom and love are both engaged in the best manner for them. Their trials do not come at random; *the very hairs of* (their) *head are all numbered.*

As the lady was leaving the shop, the silversmith called her back. He had forgotten to mention that he only knows when the process of purifying is complete by seeing his own image reflected in the silver.

1. Can you think of a time God allowed you to be in the Refiner's furnace? List at least one way in which you emerged more like the Saviour than you were prior to the refining process.

As we wrap up our study this week, I would like to share one more time the Bible uses the word "mirror" and see what we can learn from it today.

In 1 Corinthians 13:8-13 we read: *"Charity never faileth: but whether there be prophecies, they shall fail; whether there be tongues, they shall cease; whether there be knowledge, it shall vanish away. For we know in part, and we prophesy in part. But when that which is perfect is come, then that which is in part shall be done away. When I was a child, I spake as a child, I understood as a child, I thought as a child: but when I became a man, I put away childish things. For now we see through a glass, darkly; but then face to face: now I know in part; but then shall I know even as also I am known. And now abideth faith, hope, charity, these three; but the greatest of these is charity."*

The phrase *"through a glass, darkly"* is referring to a smoky mirror. All of us have experienced this when stepping out of the shower to a fogged mirror. It is hard to see our image clearly. While we live here on earth it is often hard to see the "whys" of life clearly. Why did God create me as He did? Why did God give me this deformity? Why did He allow this change in my appearance? What is the purpose for the bullying and ridicule I have suffered because of my appearance? While I wish I could answer these questions for you, I look forward to the day when we will meet face to face with the One Who does have all of the answers. I simply desire to help you put away childish thinking about your appearance and grow in your understanding of the principles found in the Word of God.

The last verse in Chapter 13 says: *"And now abideth faith, hope, charity, these three; but the greatest of these is charity."* Faith is an intangible. We cannot see it and often find ourselves at a loss to explain it. We know faith does not end when we place our reliance upon God for salvation; but rather it begins with salvation. I once heard it explained like this: "Faith is not just believing God no matter what the circumstances; but faith is obeying God no matter what the consequences." One day we will see Jesus face to face, and there will be no further need for faith, as He will reveal Himself to us.

Hope is another intangible. Hope is an expectation or a confidence. One day, Jesus will keep His promise to come again and receive us unto Himself, to take us to the place He has prepared for us, so that where He is there we may be also (John 14:2-3). One day our hope will be fulfilled and fully realized.

Charity is also an intangible, and yet we see it in God's gift to us. *"Herein is love, not that we loved God, but that the He loved us, and sent his Son to be the propitiation* (atonement or sacrifice that satisfies) *for our sins"* (1 John 4:10). We see it in the application of 1 Corinthians 13. Charity will never pass away, but will become more clearly realized as we *"grow in grace, and in the knowledge of our Lord and Saviour Jesus Christ"* (2 Pet. 3:18a).

Read the following verses, and answer the questions below:

1. According to John 13:34, what are we to do because of God's love for us?

2. According to John 15:9-10, how can we abide in God's love for us?

3. According to John 15:13, what did Jesus do as our friend to prove His love for us?

As we close this first week's study, I would like to share the following words from a song written by Norman J. Clayton back in the 1940's:

If We Could See Beyond Today

If we could see beyond today
As God can see,
If all the clouds should roll away,
The shadows flee;
O'er present griefs we would not fret,
Each sorrow we would soon forget,
For many joys are waiting yet
For you and me.

If we could know beyond today
As God doth know,
Why dearest treasures pass away,
And tears must flow;
And why the darkness leads to light,
Why dreary days will soon grow bright,
Some day life's wrong will be made right,
Faith tells us so.

If we could see, if we could know
We often say,
But God in love a veil doth throw
Across our way.
We cannot see what lies before,
And so we cling to Him the more,
He leads us till this life is o'er,
Trust and obey.

Are you willing to simply trust and obey? Are you ready to simply trust and obey?

Week Two

Lord, I Believe; Help Thou Mine Unbelief

Something to Think About

Three and a half months after my brain surgery, the lower third part of the paralyzed side of my face began to wake up. I was so excited to have my smile back again, but that excitement lessened as I began to notice something was not right. My surgeon explained to me that since my brain was unable to send messages through my facial nerves to my facial muscles, they had begun to atrophy. For those of you who like to fish, or who accompany others who like to fish, I can explain it like this. It is as though someone caught the right side of my mouth with a fish hook, pulled the fishing line up, tied it to my right ear causing my face to be pulled toward the right side and making my cheek bone appear to be swollen. I lost the normal symmetry a face should have since I had actually traded one deformity for another. Now I do want to say it was a good trade as this deformity was not nearly as noticeable as the first.

In the first three months after surgery, I dreaded going out into public because I felt the need to explain what happened to me to everyone with whom I did business. Thankfully, my husband did most of the talking, such as asking for a booth in a restaurant, since eating was extremely embarrassing for me. He would also ask for extra napkins, A LOT of extra napkins. Now that I have almost mastered eating with one or two napkins, he often tells me, "You are doing so well keeping the food in your mouth!" Sometimes you just have to go with it and laugh.

Our very first outing was a trip to the eye doctor to learn about the damage to my eye and the steps we would need to take to bring some relief and healing. I had been given a gift card to a local restaurant, so we followed the doctor's appointment with a lunch date. I remember telling my family that the stares from people were really difficult for me. I needed to use a walker for my balance, my face was terribly distorted, and, when I tried to smile at people, it only made the distortion even more pronounced. I felt particularly sorry for the little children whom I may have scared rather than consoled with my smile. Of course, we had a good laugh when we got home, and I realized my eye was Easter egg yellow from the dye needed to examine it. No wonder people were staring!

However, I did notice three ways in which people reacted to me. First there was that large group of people who looked at me and then quickly turned away. Then there was a smaller group of people consisting primarily of children and far too many adults who simply stared. Lastly, there was that wonderful group of people who did not turn away, but actually chose to interact with me. Prior to my surgery I was accustomed to being part of that last group. After all, I am a pastor's wife, and I was in the habit of reaching out to people, but after surgery my handicaps were so encompassing it was hard to reach out. My balance was off; I could not see clearly because of the ointment in my eye; I could not hear well due to my deaf ear; and I was extremely self-conscious about my facial distortion. Three of those are valid handicaps which cause us to make some adjustments before being able to reach out to others, but an undesirable appearance is NOT a valid excuse for not reaching out to others.

It was my responsibility to be sure my husband and daughter were prepared to witness to my nurses and caretakers when I was too sick to do so myself. Fortunately, I had a great example to follow from a friend who has gone through multiple surgeries. She makes up little baggies that include a gospel tract, lotion or hand sanitizer, and some treats to give out to her nurses and caregivers. I did not go to that length, but I did buy good quality chocolates and some "thank you" butter mints to place in a basket. Then I chose a gospel tract written by another friend when she was battling stage-four cancer as I felt this would be appropriate for medical workers. We placed them all together in a nice basket that my husband and daughter could offer to my nurses and caregivers. When I was discharged, we left the basket at the nurses' station for which they were very grateful. It was also my responsibility to witness to my therapists, since I was the one interacting with each of them. Fortunately for me, it was easy as I learned both of them knew the Lord.

When my face began to wake up and move upward due to the atrophy, several things were said to me by my friends and acquaintances; the most memorable statement was, "You're back to normal!" I was nowhere close to being "back to normal;" however, I was thankful for a change that was less noticeable and even appeared to some to be back to normal. I have learned not to become too upset with things that are said to me when I am going through a trial. Many years ago, the Lord taught me a valuable lesson about human nature. The year was 1988, and I was 31 years old. Due to complications in prematurely delivering our youngest child, I was given nineteen units of blood and six units of platelets. The many doctors who worked to try to save my life said there was no earthly reason for me to be alive. Our baby also received blood transfusions and spent several weeks in the neonatal intensive care unit. When baby Jack and I were finally able to return to church, I came face to face with humanity. If someone asked me how I was doing, and I answered truthfully, I was most often met with a kind reminder that I needed to be thankful both my son and I were alive. However, if someone asked me how I was doing, and I answered with how thankful I was my son and I were alive, I was most often met with a kind reminder that I needed to take care of myself because I had been to death's door and back, and I should call if I needed anything. I know this is probably terrible, but I made a game out of it. Doing so kept me from allowing the responses to hurt my feelings, and it allowed me to see how truly helpful people want to be when we choose not to make a situation all about ourselves.

Now you may be thinking, "People can be so insensitive," and I would agree with that, but I do not believe it is intentional. How often have you attended a ladies' meeting where the speaker addressed how different we all are? We have been told there are four basic temperaments. Our personalities have been compared to four different colors. I have even seen that our personalities can be compared to 16 different animals. Now, if we really believe people are so different, why do we expect them all to act the way we would when it comes to a trial in our lives? Years ago, a friend shared the following statement with me: "Your perception of me is a reflection of you; my reaction to you is an awareness of me." Often when we make a judgement about why someone did what they did to us, or said what they said to us, it is as if we are looking into a mirror at ourselves, because we are making that judgement based upon our perceptions. The way we react to the things that are done or said to us is a good indication of our spiritual condition.

Going through a trial that causes a change in our appearance is very personal, and naturally we can become very sensitive to what is done, or said, to us. Therefore, it is very important we choose to believe the best in others, even if that is not what is perceived. We cannot allow ourselves to focus on the hurtful things that are done or said to us. Rather we must focus on what we know to be true about our God. Why is this so important? Our behavior consists of our thoughts, words, and actions, and we will eventually behave according to what we believe and what we desire. We often attempt to change our behavior by simply addressing our behavior. For instance, let us say that because you do not feel attractive, you do not take opportunities to witness to those with whom you interact. You can fill your purse with gospel tracts, dress your best, and clean up as nicely as possible; however, these actions will not change your silent witness behavior. Making a change in your thinking about your responsibility to witness, and a confidence in God's wisdom in creating you as you are will, however, change your silent witness behavior.

In Proverbs 23:7 we are told: *"For as he thinketh in his heart, so is he..."* In Chapter 4 and verse 23, we are admonished to *"Keep thy heart* (thoughts) *with all diligence; for out of it are the issues of life."* And most would be familiar with the challenge in Romans 12:2: *"And be not conformed to this world: but be ye transformed by the renewing of your mind..."* You may have already formed an opinion about what you see when you look into the mirror, but at the end of Week One, I asked you if you were willing to trust and obey. It is now time for us to look into the mirror of God's Word and to begin the transformation by the renewing of our minds.

The word "believe" in the Greek means "to be persuaded, to place confidence in, to trust, or to rely upon." One of the Greek words for "faith" is actually translated "belief." In the next three days, we are going to look at three words: believe, trust, and faith. If I were to ask you, "What is it about God that causes you to be able to place your confidence in Him," what would your answer be? Below I have listed various names of our God. Read through the list, and choose at least three with which you are the least familiar, or that interest you the most, then read the Scripture texts associated with them. Once you have completed this assignment, revisit the question, "What is it about God that causes me to be able to place my confidence in Him?"

- Adonai means "The Lord", and it represents God as Authority, the One Whom we obey. (Ps. 8; Matt. 28:18; 1 Tim. 6:14-16)

- El is found as a prefix to several of the names of God, and alone it simply means "The Strong One." (Num. 23:22; Deut. 7:9)

- El Elohe Yisreal means "God, The God of Israel." (Ex. 5:1; Ps. 106:48)

- El Elyon means "The God Most High." (Ps. 57:2, 78:35; Dan. 4:34)

- Elohim means "The All-Powerful God." (Gen. 1:1-3, 26)

- El Olam means "The Eternal or Everlasting God." (Ps. 90:1-2; Isa. 40:28)

- El Roi means "The God Who Sees Me." (Gen. 16:11-13; Ps. 34:15,139:7-12)

- El Shaddai means "The God Almighty." (Gen. 17:1; Ps. 90:2, 91:1)

- Immanuel means "God with Us." (Isa. 7:14; Matt. 1:23)

- Jehovah (Also YHWH pronounced YAH-way) means "The unchanging, eternal, self-existing God, the I Am that I Am." It is important to remember the name "Jehovah" is not a title, but rather the personal, proper name of God, signifying God's desire to have a personal relationship with His people. It is not used in the New Testament, because Jesus is the embodiment of Jehovah, and His name means "Jehovah is Salvation." (Ex. 6:3; Ps. 83:18; Isa.12:2)

- Jehovah-Jireh means "The Lord Will Provide." (Gen. 22:13-14)

- Jehovah-Mekaddishkem means "The Lord Who Sanctifies." (Ex. 31:12-13)

- Jehovah-Nissi means "The Lord Is My Banner." (Ex. 17:15-16; Isa. 11:10-12)

- Jehovah-Rapha means "The Lord Who Heals." (Ex. 15:25-27; Ps. 103:3, 147:3)

- Jehovah-Rohi means "The Lord Is My Shepherd." (Ps. 23; Is. 40:11; John 10:1-18)

- Jehovah-Sabaoth means "The Lord of Hosts." (1 Sam. 17:45; Isa. 47:4; Ps. 46:7)

- Jehovah-Shalom means "The Lord Is Peace." (Judg. 6:22-24; Isa. 9:6)

- Jehovah-Shammah means "The Lord Is There." (Ezek. 48:35; Ps. 46)

- Jehovah-Tsidkenu means "The Lord Our Righteousness." (Jer. 23:5-6; Ps. 145:17)

As I was writing this list, I could not help but feel somewhat humbled. Who am I to tell the Almighty, Eternal, All-Powerful God how He should have created me? Who am I to question the circumstances in my life allowed by my Provider, my Healer, my Good Shepherd, my Immanuel who promises to never leave me nor forsake me (Heb. 13:5)? No one else is known by so many names. Not only can we believe in our God, but we can also believe our God.

Now we will take a look at the word "trust." There were several meanings for the word "trust," and because Proverbs 3:5 is such a popular verse, I have chosen to use that definition for today's lesson. *"Trust* (to confide, to place hope and confidence in anyone, to be confident, to be secure without fear) *in the LORD with all thine heart; and lean not unto thine own understanding."* I found it interesting that in almost all of the meanings for the word "trust" we find the definition "to confide in." I find this to be so precious. You will have loved ones who will do their best to try to understand what you are going through, but, at some point, you may feel very alone. Because God promised, *"I will never leave thee, nor forsake thee"* (Heb. 13:5), we can believe He is always with us. Not only is He there, but we can confide in Him those things that are just too personal to share with anyone else.

Yesterday, we looked at the names of our God. Today, I would like us to look at some of the attributes of God. Read through the list, and choose at least three with which you are the least familiar, or that interest you the most, then read the Scripture texts associated with them. Once you have completed this assignment, take a few minutes to write down how these attributes help you in being able to trust Him.

- God is faithful. (Deut. 7:9; Isa. 49:7-8; 1 Cor. 1:9, 10:13; 1 Pet. 4:19; Ps. 119:75; Lam. 3:22-23)

- God is good. (Ps. 25:7, 27:13, 31:19, 34:8, 52:1, 107:8; Rom. 2:2-4)

- God is gracious. (Joel 2:12-14; Jonah 4:2; John 1:14-18; 1 Pet. 2:1-3)

- God is holy. (Ps. 30:4, 47:8, 99:9; Rom. 1:3-7)

- God is immutable, or never changing; He does not get any better than this. (Mal. 3:6; Heb. 13:8)

- God is just. (Ps. 94; Rev. 15:3-4)

- God is love. (1 John 4:7-19)

- God is merciful. (Luke 6:36; Titus 3:5; Heb. 8:12; 1 Pet. 1:3)

- God is omnipotent or all-powerful. (Ps. 62:11; Rev. 19:6)

- God is omnipresent or everywhere. (Ps. 139:1-18)

- God is omniscient or all-knowing. (Isa. 40:13-14, 28; Rom. 11:33-34; 1 Cor. 2:11)

- God is transcendent or surpassing all limits. (Isa. 57:15)

- God is wise. (Job 12:9-13, 28:12-28; Prov. 3:19-23; 1 Tim. 1:17; Rev. 7:12)

Finally, we will look at the word "faith." In Hebrews 11:6 we read: *"But without faith it is impossible to please him: for he that cometh to God must believe that he is, and that he is a rewarder of them that diligently seek him."* The meaning of the word "faith" in Hebrews 11 is the primary meaning of faith throughout the New Testament. It is a conviction of the truth, or a belief that includes trust. On Day 7 of Week 1, I shared a statement I heard years ago regarding faith. "Faith is not just believing God no matter what the circumstances, but faith is obeying God no matter what the consequences." Perhaps there is no greater chapter in the Bible about faith than Hebrews Chapter 11. It has been referred to as the "Great Hall of Faith." Today, I would like us to witness faith in action. Read Hebrews Chapter 11, and make note of each person mentioned and their acts of obedience in spite of the consequences they faced. If you do not get through the entire chapter today, you may want to revisit this chapter in the near future as some of the most convicting verses are near the end of the chapter. In a recent sermon preached by my husband the following statement was made: "Do not judge God by your circumstances, but rather judge your circumstances by God." I cannot help but think of the men and women of faith in Chapter 11 who chose to do just that.

1. Is there a circumstance in your life where you have been tempted to judge God?

2. How has the testimony of the believers in Hebrews Chapter 11 given you a different outlook on your circumstance?

Now that we have taken a few days to look at the many reasons why we can believe God, why we can trust our God, and what it means to have faith in God, I would like us to take the next three days to apply these truths to His plan for us.

First of all, we need to look at a couple of passages that make it clear God was intricately involved in our creation. Please consider with me Psalm 139:13-16 where the Psalmist states: *"For thou hast possessed my reins: thou hast covered me in my mother's womb. I will praise thee; for I am fearfully and wonderfully made: marvellous are thy works; and that my soul knoweth right well. My substance was not hid from thee, when I was made in secret, and curiously wrought in the lowest parts of the earth. Thine eyes did see my substance, yet being unperfect; and in thy book all my members were written, which in continuance were fashioned, when as yet there was none of them."*

Now consider Isaiah 43:7: *"Even every one that is called by my name: for I have created him for my glory, I have formed him; yea, I have made him."* The word "created" has to do with our conception, and the word "formed" is talking about our physical attributes. According to this verse, we were created as we are so we may bring glory to God. The word "glory" means to "magnify, extol, praise." Our very creation is an opportunity to show the world what God is like. We were made to show what God can do in and with a life like ours.

Please allow me to illustrate this thought for you. If you were to come to our home, you would see many decorations throughout our home that I have created. There are some that are quite large, others that are quite small, and some that are just average. They also come in various shapes and color schemes to fit the various purposes I have for them. Some of them required more hot glue than others in order to make them the creation of beauty they are to me. I did not apply the hot glue because I did not like that particular decoration; I applied the hot glue to make it beautiful. Some of my decorations have a place of prominence as they hang in our living room where everyone can see them. Others hang in our downstairs guest room where only those who spend the night will see them. Still others are seasonal and are only seen one to three months a year.

If you were to come visit our home you might not like my taste in decorations, but that is simply your opinion based upon your various likes and dislikes. I love my decorations. I am the creator; I made what I wanted and what I needed. Each of my decorations is important to me. The decorations that hang in the guest room are no less important to me than those that hang in our living room. The seasonal decorations used for a few short months are no less important to me than the ones I use year-round. My decorations show off what I can do as the creator, and so it is with God. Each of us was specifically created to bring glory to God.

Have you ever taken the time to really look at yourself? I am not referring to the reflection you see when you look into a mirror; I am referring to the unique way in which God created you. Today, I would like you to take a few minutes to write down the various attributes, talents, and abilities God has given you. Beside each one list the ways in which you are using your attributes, talents, and abilities for God's glory. If you come across one which you are not using, think of some possible ways God could use this for His glory. I have given you an example of each of these from my own life to help you get started.

1. An attribute is a quality or characteristic of a person, and it refers to our character. God has created me with the character quality of orderliness. One of my favorite verses is 1 Corinthians 14:40: *"Let all things be done decently and in order."* I use this character trait in organizing various events at our church, in organizing our storage closet, and in organizing our shed, so the items are kept neatly and ready for use. On the next page record the attribute(s) that God has given to you.

2. A talent is a natural aptitude or skill. While we may have received some instruction, this is something that comes easily to us. God has given me the talent of being able to see things that need to be cleaned, and I use this talent each time I clean the downstairs area of our church building. What talent(s) has God given you?

3. An ability is a skill which is learned over time and with some effort on our part. God has given me an ability in sewing, and I use this ability to help ladies dress in a way that is modest; whether that means fixing a neckline, fixing a hem, sewing up a slit, or various other needs. What ability or abilities has God given you?

Once you have taken a good look at yourself, you can use this information to identify your spiritual gift(s). God has given each of us spiritual gifts to be used for His service in our local churches. If you have not already identified your spiritual gift(s), you may want to take the information you have written in your answers above to your pastor and pastor's wife. Then they can help you find the area of service which would be most suitable to the attributes, talents, and abilities God has given you.

Perhaps the verse God used the most to change my thinking about the way in which He created me is found in Revelation 4:11: *"Thou art worthy, O Lord, to receive glory and honour and power: for thou hast created all things, and for thy pleasure they are and were created."* The word "pleasure" here means "for God's will." Each and every creation came about because God wanted it. I absolutely love the thought that God created me for His pleasure. He wanted me, so He created me exactly the way He wanted me. After learning this truth, I have often stopped to ask myself, "Am I pleasing the Lord?"

Read the following Scripture passages about pleasing God, then use your own words to apply them to your life.

1. Psalm 51:17-19

2. Psalm 147:10-11

3. Micah 6:6-8

4. Romans 8:6-9

5. 2 Timothy 2:1-4

Take joy, my friend, in knowing you were created for God's pleasure. Stop and meditate on this precious thought.

As we close out this week, I would like to take just a moment and look at the danger of not believing God. In Numbers 20:7-12 we read a very sad story: *"And the LORD spake unto Moses, saying, Take the rod, and gather thou the assembly together, thou, and Aaron thy brother, and speak ye unto the rock before their eyes; and it shall give forth his water, and thou shalt bring forth to them water out of the rock: so thou shalt give the congregation and their beasts drink. And Moses took the rod from before the LORD, as he commanded him. And Moses and Aaron gathered the congregation together before the rock, and he said unto them, Hear now, ye rebels; must we fetch you water out of this rock? And Moses lifted up his hand, and with his rod he smote the rock twice: and the water came out abundantly, and the congregation drank, and their beasts also. And the LORD spake unto Moses and Aaron, Because ye believed me not, to sanctify me in the eyes of the children of Israel, therefore ye shall not bring this congregation into the land which I have given them."*

In Hebrews Chapter 11, we witnessed the faith of Moses as God listed several of his acts of obedience, but, in Numbers, we find an act of disobedience that cost him dearly. I would imagine he was pretty tired of this group of whining, disgruntled followers; nevertheless, God had given him an instruction to follow, and he chose to do it differently. He did not get to enter the Promised Land in spite of the many years of leadership he had provided to these followers, but God in His mercy did allow him to see it. Moses knew God; he spent time in the very presence of God; yet, in a careless moment, he acted inconsistently with what he knew to be true about God. *"...For unto whomsoever much is given, of him shall be much required..."* (Luke 12:48).

Choose one of the three following women, and read the account of her actions that resulted from her failure to believe God. Record the consequences of her disbelief below.

1. Eve (Gen. 2:15-3:24)

2. Sarah (Gen. 15:5-16:16; 17:15-22; 21:1-21)

3. Rebekah (Gen. 25:20-34; 27:1-25)

Unbelief is a choice we make anytime we refuse to believe what God says is true. You, too, may have a beautiful sister who seems to have all of the attributes you wish for yourself, and you may be tempted to think, "God sure does love her and has a purpose for her, but not me." The names of God, the attributes of God, and the truths regarding the very character of our God are not just true for a few; they are truth. In John 8:28-32 we read: *"Then said Jesus unto them,*

When ye have lifted up the Son of man, then shall ye know that I am he, and that I do nothing of myself; but as my Father hath taught me, I speak these things. And he that sent me is with me: the Father hath not left me alone; for I do always those things that please him. As he spake these words, many believed on him. Then said Jesus to those Jews which believed on him, If ye continue in my word, then are ye my disciples indeed; And ye shall know the truth, and the truth shall make you free."

4. What truth have you learned this week that has caused you to believe differently about the way God has created you, or about the circumstance He has allowed into your life that has altered your appearance?

In Mark 9:21-27, we read another story of a man struggling with what he believed: *"And he asked his father, How long is it ago since this came unto him? And he said, Of a child. And ofttimes it hath cast him into the fire, and into the waters, to destroy him: but if thou canst do any thing, have compassion on us, and help us. Jesus said unto him, If thou canst believe, all things are possible to him that believeth. And straightway the father of the child cried out, and said with tears, Lord, I believe; help thou mine unbelief. When Jesus saw that the people came running together, he rebuked the foul spirit, saying unto him, Thou dumb and deaf spirit, I charge thee, come out of him, and enter no more into him. And the spirit cried, and rent him sore, and came out of him: and he was as one dead; insomuch that many said, He is dead. But Jesus took him by the hand, and lifted him up; and he arose."*

Do you not love this father's honesty as he proclaims his belief in Jesus' ability to heal his son, while admitting his lack of faith, but sharing his desire to have that faith strengthened? Perhaps as we come to the end of this week, you are also thinking, *"Lord I believe; help thou mine unbelief."* Romans 10:17 gives us the remedy for having our faith strengthened: *"So then faith cometh by hearing, and hearing by the word of God."* If there is one chapter in this book you may want to refer back to often, it is this chapter. It would be good at some point to read all of the names and attributes of God and the Scripture texts associated with them. Your pastor may even have additional studies for you to consider. The Psalms is a wonderful book for growing your faith in the kind of God we have. Take the time to mark each time the Psalmist says, *"He is my..."* or *"The Lord is my..."* We can also see the character of God in the life of Christ, so another great place to build your faith in the kind of God we have is to make a study of the life of Christ in the Gospels.

Remember, we will all eventually behave according to what we believe and what we desire. If you desire to have an accurate belief about our God, to trust Him fully, and to have a faith that pleases Him, you will take the next step in getting to know Him better. As we leave this week and enter the next, it would be good to pray Psalm 139:23-24: *"Search me, O God, and know my heart: try me, and know my thoughts: And see if there be any wicked way in me, and lead me in the way everlasting."* Next, we are going to take an honest look at what we really desire.

Week Three

What Do You Really Want?

Something to Think About

At my eight-month post-operative appointment, my surgeon confirmed that the middle third part of my face had awakened. When it did, it revealed a neurological symptom known as Synkinesis: a condition which causes abnormal, involuntary facial movement to occur with the voluntary movement of different facial muscle groups. It is the result of the mis-wiring of the facial nerves after the trauma of surgery. In my case, it causes my right eye to close whenever I use the muscle in my right cheek. I had grown accustomed to my crooked smile, but this condition causes me to appear to be in agony when I smile. Although I dreaded having to wear glasses again, I was thankful because they seemed to mask the condition of my eye. Some people did not notice any difference; however, those who are the closest to me noticed right away. Their honesty was actually refreshing because I knew they would see the need for me to allow God to once again do a work in my heart. Many years ago, I claimed Ephesians 3:20: *"Now unto him that is able to do exceeding abundantly above all that we ask or think, according to the power that worketh in us."* However, I did not claim it in its context. While I do believe God can *"do exceeding abundantly above all that we ask or think,"* the context of this verse is that He is able to do in our hearts what we may believe is impossible. His grace truly is sufficient! *"For this thing I besought the Lord thrice, that it might depart from me. And he said unto me, My grace is sufficient for thee: for my strength is made perfect in weakness. Most gladly therefore will I rather glory in my infirmities, that the power of Christ may rest upon me"* (2 Cor. 12:8).

With this new condition, I once again faced the choice to believe what I know to be true about God and trust Him, or allow this change to discourage me. I decided to choose to remember what He had done for me in the past and to once again rest in the knowledge of His loving-kindness. The children of Israel were faced with this same choice over and over again. In Psalm 78, God recorded for us their struggle to trust Him, a list of His acts they had forgotten, and their sin of unbelief. The same chapter, however, ends very sweetly with the following words: *So he fed them according to the integrity of his heart; and guided them by the skilfulness of his hands* (vs. 72). How precious that our God cared for them as He did! They did not deserve it, but because of His integrity, He cared for their needs. Later, in Psalm 106, we see the acknowledgement and confession of the sins of Israel. This chapter records both God's acts and Israel's sins, but I want to point out verse fifteen where the Bible says: *"And he gave them their request; but sent leanness into their soul."* According to this verse, God gave them their desires, in spite of the fact it was obviously not His perfect will for them.

The Merriam-Webster Dictionary defines the word "desire" as something for which we long or hope. A desire comes when we recognize a need in our lives, whether that need is genuine or simply one that is perceived. Since I desire to be a help to my husband in our ministry, I felt it was a genuine need for God to allow me to regain my balance so I would be able to function on my own again. I also felt it was a genuine need for God to heal my eye so it would once again be safe for me to drive. While I believed these were genuine needs, I must tell you, I also humbled myself before the Lord realizing He may have a different plan for me. We will address this further next week.

Each of us has the ability to grow our desires by increasing the amount of time we spend thinking about them. Perhaps you can relate to me in my desire for all things dark chocolate. My favorite treats change regularly, and during this trial in my life, I fell in love with the Russell Stover dark chocolate mints. It was quite helpful that I could purchase a small bag for one dollar at the Dollar Tree, conveniently located less than a mile from our home. When the desire for a dark chocolate mint enters my mind, I have a choice to make. Is this desire a genuine or perceived need? It would be wise for me to think about the results of eating that dark chocolate mint knowing it is impossible for me to eat just one. I must remind myself that if I choose to indulge, I will not be happy the next time I step on the scale. Reminding myself this is not a genuine need will help me not to succumb to the temptation. However, if I reject this truth and allow myself to think about the creamy, buttery, mint filling, the rich, dark chocolate coating, how long it has been since I have enjoyed one, or how inexpensive they are, I am simply growing my desire and will probably hop in my car and drive to the Dollar Tree to indulge.

Choosing not to believe what God says in His Word leads us to have sinful desires. We then allow ourselves to believe the lie that God is not enough for us, nor is He doing enough for us. James 1:14 and 15 give us the progression of the downward spiral from desire to sin. *"But every man is tempted, when he is drawn away of his own lust* (desire), *and enticed* (to be caught by bait). *Then when lust hath conceived, it bringeth forth sin: and sin, when it is finished, bringeth forth death."* Since we cannot be tempted by things we do not desire, the best way to fight temptation is to change our desires. I did not know God's will regarding what was happening to my face. I honestly did not believe having my face restored to its pre-surgical condition was a need, so I made the decision not to spend a great deal of time looking at my reflection in the mirror, nor begging God to restore my face to its pre-surgical condition. I did not want to grow a desire that may not be God's will for me.

Early in my recovery, I came across Psalm 17:15, and it captured my heart. The Psalmist expressed his desire when he said, *"…I shall be satisfied, when I awake, with thy likeness."* Perhaps as we look into our mirrors, choose a lotion, make-up, and a hairstyle, it would behoove us to ask ourselves if we awoke with His likeness. In Week One we learned that it is His will for us to be conformed to His image, but sadly, many of us desire to wake up with the beauty dictated by the world's standards rather than with a likeness to Christ.

This week I hope to challenge you with regard to your desires, and to encourage you to desire to be like Jesus. We will also look at the lives of some women who chose to live with His likeness.

To Be Like Jesus, To Be Like Jesus
(Author Unknown)

To be like Jesus, to be like Jesus,
All I ask to be like Him;
All through life's journey
From earth to glory
All I ask to be like Him;

To be like Jesus, to be like Jesus,
All I ask to be like Him;
Not in a measure
but in its fullness
All I ask to be like Him.

In Luke 4:1 we read: *"And Jesus being full of the Holy Ghost returned from Jordan, and was led by the Spirit into the wilderness."* Of course, the context of this verse is Jesus being led by the Spirit into a situation where He would be tempted by Satan. This teaches us a very important lesson we will look at more closely on Day 3. In Hebrews 1:9 we read: *"Thou hast loved righteousness, and hated iniquity; therefore God, even thy God, hath anointed thee with the oil of gladness above thy fellows."* This is a direct reference to the Messianic prophecy found in Psalm 45:7: *"Thou lovest righteousness, and hatest wickedness: therefore God, thy God, hath anointed thee with the oil of gladness above thy fellows."* Then in Acts 10:38 we read: *"How God anointed Jesus of Nazareth with the Holy Ghost and with power: who went about doing good, and healing all that were oppressed of the devil; for God was with him."*

Being filled with, or led by the Spirit is one of the basics of the Christian life, and yet we often overlook its importance in our lives. The Word of God teaches that walking in the Spirit is the antidote for not fulfilling the lusts, or desires of our flesh. *"This I say then, Walk in the Spirit, and ye shall not fulfil the lust of the flesh. For the flesh lusteth against the Spirit, and the Spirit against the flesh: and these are contrary the one to the other: so that ye cannot do the things that ye would"* (Gal. 5:16-17).

In connection with this line of thinking, I recently heard a suggestion from Dr. Terry Coomer, founder and director of Hope Biblical Counseling Center, for applying 1 John 2:15-17 in our lives. *"Love not the world, neither the things that are in the world. If any man love the world, the love of the Father is not in him. For all that is in the world, the lust of the flesh* (an intense desire to do something), *and the lust of the eyes* (an intense desire to have something), *and the pride of life* (an intense desire to be something), *is not of the Father, but is of the world.*" Dr. Coomer suggested going on the offensive in the battle with our lusts (strong desires) each day by asking the Holy Spirit the following three questions: What do you want me to do today? What do you want me to have today? What do you want me to be today?

The evidence of being filled with, or controlled by the Holy Spirit is found in Galatians 5:22-26: *"But the fruit of the Spirit is love, joy, peace, longsuffering, gentleness, goodness, faith, meekness, temperance: against such there is no law. And they that are Christ's have crucified the flesh with the affections and lusts. If we live in the Spirit, let us also walk in the Spirit. Let us not be desirous of vain glory, provoking one another, envying one another."* We can act lovingly, joyfully, peacefully, etcetera, but only for a limited amount of time. Often, the trials that come into our lives reveal to us our sin nature and our need to wholly depend upon the Lord for His control. We must ask ourselves: do I desire to be filled with, that is controlled by the Holy Spirit?

Read Luke 1:5-17, 41-45, and answer the questions below:

1. How does God describe Elisabeth?

2. What does He say about her physical appearance?

In John 1:1 we read: *"In the beginning was the Word, and the Word was with God, and the Word was God."* In 1 John 5:7 we read: *"For there are three that bear record in heaven, the Father, the Word, and the Holy Ghost: and these three are one."* Here we find Jesus being referred to as *"the Word."* On Day Two, we mentioned Jesus being led by the Spirit into the wilderness, and Luke 4:2-13 gives us the rest of this story: *"Being forty days tempted of the devil. And in those days he did eat nothing: and when they were ended, he afterward hungered. And the devil said unto him, If thou be the Son of God, command this stone that it be made bread. And Jesus answered him, saying, It is written, That man shall not live by bread alone, but by every word of God. And the devil, taking him up into an high mountain, shewed unto him all the kingdoms of the world in a moment of time. And the devil said unto him, All this power will I give thee, and the glory of them: for that is delivered unto me; and to whomsoever I will I give it. If thou therefore wilt worship me, all shall be thine. And Jesus answered and said unto him, Get thee behind me, Satan: for it is written, Thou shalt worship the Lord thy God, and him only shalt thou serve. And he brought him to Jerusalem, and set him on a pinnacle of the temple, and said unto him, If thou be the Son of God, cast thyself down from hence: For it is written, He shall give his angels charge over thee, to keep thee: And in their hands they shall bear thee up, lest at any time thou dash thy foot against a stone. And Jesus answering said unto him, It is said, Thou shalt not tempt the Lord thy God. And when the devil had ended all the temptation, he departed from him for a season."* Jesus resisted each of these temptations from Satan with the Word of God.

In Colossians 3:16-23 we read: *"Let the word of Christ dwell in you richly in all wisdom; teaching and admonishing one another in psalms and hymns and spiritual songs, singing with grace in your hearts to the*

Lord. And whatsoever ye do in word or deed, do all in the name of the Lord Jesus, giving thanks to God and the Father by him. Wives, submit yourselves unto your own husbands, as it is fit in the Lord. Husbands, love your wives, and be not bitter against them. Children, obey your parents in all things: for this is well pleasing unto the Lord. Fathers, provoke not your children to anger, lest they be discouraged. Servants, obey in all things your masters according to the flesh; not with eyeservice, as menpleasers; but in singleness of heart, fearing God: And whatsoever ye do, do it heartily, as to the Lord, and not unto men." This is a parallel passage to Ephesians 5:18-6:9; however, in Ephesians 5, our passage begins with, *"And be not drunk with wine, wherein is excess; but be filled with the Spirit; Speaking to yourselves in psalms and hymns and spiritual songs, singing and making melody in your heart to the Lord..."* These two passages show us the evidences of being filled with the Spirit, along with revealing to us our need to be filled with the Word of God in order to be filled with the Spirit.

Psalm 19:7-11 is a popular Scripture song with which many of us are familiar, but I wonder how many times we have sung these words without giving any real thought to what they actually mean. *"The law of the LORD is perfect, converting the soul: the testimony of the LORD is sure, making wise the simple. The statutes of the LORD are right, rejoicing the heart: the commandment of the LORD is pure, enlightening the eyes. The fear of the LORD is clean, enduring for ever: the judgments of the LORD are true and righteous altogether. More to be desired are they than gold, yea, than much fine gold: sweeter also than honey and the honeycomb. Moreover by them is thy servant warned: and in keeping of them there is great reward."* We must ask ourselves: do I desire to live my life in accordance to the Word of God?

Read Acts 18:24-28 and Romans 16:3-4, then answer the following questions:

1. How does God describe Priscilla?

2. What does He say about her physical appearance?

In Luke 6:12 we read: *"And it came to pass in those days, that he went out into a mountain to pray, and continued all night in prayer to God."* Then in Luke 9:28-29 we see another example of how spending time with God altered even Jesus' appearance. *"And it came to pass about an eight days after these sayings, he took Peter and John and James, and went up into a mountain to pray. And as he prayed, the fashion of his countenance was altered, and his raiment was white and glistering."* Peter, John, and James were so blessed to have been able to witness the communion between God the Father and God the Son, and then to also witness an exchange with two Old Testament saints. Yet even with this first-hand knowledge, they did not grasp the seriousness of the communion between Father and Son in the Garden of Gethsemane, nor were they persuaded enough to stand with Jesus in His hour of greatest need.

One of the most precious exchanges between Father and Son is recorded for us in John 17. Listen to the words of our Saviour in verses 1-8 as He tells His Father He has accomplished His task: *"These words spake Jesus, and lifted up his eyes to heaven, and said, Father, the hour is come; glorify thy Son, that thy Son also may glorify thee: As thou hast given him power over all flesh, that he should give eternal life to as many as thou hast given him. And this is life eternal, that they might know thee the only true God, and Jesus Christ, whom thou hast sent. I have glorified thee on the earth: I have finished the work which thou gavest me to do. And now, O Father, glorify thou me with thine own self with the glory which I had with thee before the world was. I have manifested thy name unto the men which thou gavest me out of the world: thine they were, and thou gavest them me; and they have kept thy word. Now they have known that all things whatsoever thou hast given me are of thee. For I have given unto them the words which thou gavest me; and they have received them, and have known surely that I came out from thee, and they have believed that thou didst send me."*

He then turned His attention to interceding for those He would leave behind and made a profound request of His Father in verses 20-23: *"Neither pray I for these alone, but for them also which shall believe on me through their word; That they all may be one; as thou, Father, art in me, and I in thee, that they also may be one in us: that the world may believe that thou hast sent me. And the glory which thou gavest me I have given them; that they may be one, even as we are one: I in them, and thou in me, that they may be made perfect in one; and that the world may know that thou hast sent me, and hast loved them, as thou hast loved me."*

One of our Saviour's last requests was for us to be able to commune with the God-head. It is also the desire of God the Father that we would commune with Him. In Exodus 25:21-22, we see His provision for Old Testament saints to be able to spend time in His presence: *"And thou shalt put the mercy seat above upon the ark; and in the ark thou shalt put the testimony that I shall give thee. And there I will meet with thee, and I will commune with thee from above the mercy seat, from between the two cherubims which are upon the ark of the testimony, of all things which I will give thee in commandment unto the children of Israel."* We must ask ourselves: do I desire to commune with God?

Read Luke 10:38-42, and answer the questions below:

1. How does God describe Mary?

2. What does He say about her physical appearance?

In John 15:12-13 we read: *"This is my commandment, That ye love one another, as I have loved you. Greater love hath no man than this, that a man lay down his life for his friends."* Jesus showed us exactly what this love looks like as He lived and died here on this earth. This kind of love is so important that we are told in Scripture that loving God is the greatest commandment, followed only by loving others as we already love ourselves. *"And Jesus answered him, The first of all the commandments is, Hear, O Israel; The Lord our God is one Lord: And thou shalt love the Lord thy God with all thy heart, and with all thy soul, and with all thy mind, and with all thy strength: this is the first commandment. And the second is like, namely this, Thou shalt love thy neighbour as thyself. There is none other commandment greater than these"* (Mark 12:29-31).

The Lord has given us one entire chapter that explains how this love should be expressed. I have added the definitions for each of these acts of love to help us gain a better understanding. *"Charity* (Agape love which does not focus on oneself but rather on the object of that love) *suffereth long* (is not easily brought to a place of resentment), *and is kind* (does good deeds); *charity envieth not* (envy is beyond jealousy; it seeks to cause the subject not to enjoy what they have); *charity vaunteth not itself* (not boastful), *is not puffed up* (prideful), *Doth not behave itself unseemly* (act unbecomingly), *seeketh not her own, is not easily provoked* (long-fused), *thinketh no evil* (does not keep a list of offenses committed); *Rejoiceth not in iniquity* (does not take pleasure in offenses committed against God), *but rejoiceth in the truth; Beareth all things* (to protect or preserve by covering), *believeth all things* (believes the best in others unless proven otherwise), *hopeth all things* (chooses to be positive and hopeful rather than critical and negative), *endureth all things* (to bear up courageously under suffering) " (1 Cor. 13:4-7). We must ask ourselves: do I desire to love as God loves?

Read Luke 7:37-50, and answer the questions below:

1. How does God describe this unnamed woman?

2. What does He say about her physical appearance?

In the previous lesson, we took note of Mary's desire to commune with Jesus. It is quite possible, as she was sitting at His feet, she heard Him relay the story of this unnamed woman and desired to follow her example in showing love to the Saviour. The cost of an alabaster box of ointment was about one year's wages for a poor person, but Mary had listened well, and then prepared to give this gift of love. Mark 14:3-9 records the account of Mary of Bethany as she follows the example of the unnamed woman in Luke Chapter 7: *"And being in Bethany in the house of Simon the leper, as he sat at meat, there came a woman having an alabaster box of ointment of spikenard very precious; and she brake the box, and poured it on his head. And there were some that had indignation within themselves, and said, Why was this waste of the ointment made? For it might have been sold for more than three hundred pence, and have been given to the poor. And they murmured against her. And Jesus said, Let her alone; why trouble ye her? she hath wrought a good work on me. For ye have the poor with you always, and whensoever ye will ye may do them good: but me ye have not always. She hath done what she could: she is come aforehand to anoint my body to the burying. Verily I say unto you, Wheresoever this gospel shall be preached throughout the whole world, this also that she hath done shall be spoken of for a memorial of her."*

We see a principle here that can help us grow our love for the Lord and for others. In Matthew 6:21 we read: *"For where your treasure is, there will your heart be also."* Our hearts will follow those areas in which we invest. If you are struggling in the area of loving God with all of your heart, soul, mind, and strength, I would challenge you to examine how much you are investing in the things of God. If you are struggling in the area of loving others, I would challenge you to examine how much of yourself you are investing in those with whom you struggle.

As we wrap up today's study, I do want to mention there has been some confusion over the comparison of loving others as we love ourselves. Nowhere in God's Word are we commanded to love ourselves because by nature we already do that. When we are cold, we turn up the heat or add another garment; when we are hot, we try to find a way to cool down; when we are hungry, we eat; when we are thirsty, we drink; when we are sad, we look for comfort; when we are happy, we look to share it with another and on and on we could go. We care for our bodies and our spirits because we love ourselves. If we are to love others as we love ourselves, we must look for ways in which we can care for the bodies and spirits of others.

I would like to leave you with the following words from our Saviour: *"For I was an hungred, and ye gave me meat: I was thirsty, and ye gave me drink: I was a stranger, and ye took me in: Naked, and ye clothed me: I was sick, and ye visited me: I was in prison, and ye came unto me. Then shall the righteous answer him, saying, Lord, when saw we thee an hungred, and fed thee? or thirsty, and gave thee drink? When saw we thee a stranger, and took thee in? or naked, and clothed thee? Or when saw we thee sick, or in prison, and came unto thee? And the King shall answer and say unto them, Verily I say unto you, Inasmuch as ye have done it unto one of the least of these my brethren, ye have done it unto me"* (Matt. 25:35-40). Again, we must ask ourselves: do I desire to love as God loves?

In 2 Timothy 2:3-4 we read: *"Thou therefore endure hardness, as a good soldier of Jesus Christ. No man that warreth entangleth himself with the affairs of this life; that he may please him who hath chosen him to be a soldier."* Jesus endured hardness from the very beginning of His life here on earth. In Matthew 8:20 we are told: *"And Jesus saith unto him, The foxes have holes, and the birds of the air have nests; but the Son of man hath not where to lay his head."* I will not take the time to go into all of the physical hardness He endured on the cross; however, I would like to address some of the emotional hardness He endured in the hours leading up to the crucifixion.

The Last Supper was attended by Jesus' disciples, His 12 closest followers. He had just shared how He was going to be betrayed, and instead of them being concerned for His well-being, they began arguing over who would be the greatest. Listen to the words from Luke 22:24: *"And there was also a strife among them, which of them should be accounted the greatest."* Then at the end of the meal, we find Jesus serving these same 12 self-centered friends. *"He riseth from supper, and laid aside his garments; and took a towel, and girded himself. After that he poureth water into a bason, and began to wash the disciples' feet, and to wipe them with the towel wherewith he was girded"* (John 13:4-5). He knew every one of them would forsake Him in His hour of greatest need, yet He still chose to humble Himself in washing their feet.

For many years, I have felt as though the scene in the Garden of Gethsemane was one of the saddest places in all of Scripture. Jesus took 12 of His followers to the garden and with three of His closest friends walked further into the garden, saying to them, *"My soul is exceeding sorrowful unto death: tarry ye here, and watch."* He then proceeded a bit further, fell to the ground, and pleaded with His Father, *"Abba, Father, all things are possible unto thee; take away this cup from me: nevertheless not what I will, but what thou wilt."* After pouring out His heart to His Father, He made His way back to the three and found them asleep. He repeated this three times, and each time He found them asleep (Mark 14:32-42). We cannot even begin to imagine the intensity with which our Saviour spoke the words, *"My soul is exceeding sorrowful."* The omniscient Son of God submitted His will to the will of His Father fully knowing the price He was about to pay. Not only did He know the physical pain He was facing, but He also knew the spiritual pain He would endure. It must have been heart-rending to realize the One with Whom He had enjoyed a sweet unity from eternity past was about to turn His back towards Him. When He prayed to the Father, He called Him "Abba Father." "Abba" was a word used by infants learning to speak and means "an unreasoning trust." When combined with the word "Father" they show the love and intelligent confidence of the child. Can you imagine the difficulty of placing loving, intelligent, unreasoning trust in our Heavenly Father when faced with certain death?

There is also the classic account of Peter's promise of faithfulness. Luke 22:33-34 says: *"And he said unto him, Lord, I am ready to go with thee, both into prison, and to death. And he said, I tell thee, Peter, the cock shall not crow this day, before that thou shalt thrice deny that thou knowest me."* Peter's betrayal began in verse fifty-four, and by the end of verse sixty-two, he was defeated, broken, and weeping bitter tears as he fled the scene. Jesus showed throughout His life here on earth how to endure hardness as a good soldier. We must ask ourselves: do I desire to be a good soldier of Jesus Christ?

1. How does God describe Deborah in Judges 4:4-9?

2. What does He say about her physical appearance?

3. How does God describe Jael in Judges 4:17-24?

4. What does He say about her physical appearance?

In Matthew 9:35 we read: *"And Jesus went about all the cities and villages, teaching in their synagogues, and preaching the gospel of the kingdom, and healing every sickness and every disease among the people."* Then in Acts 10:36-38 we read: *"The word which God sent unto the children of Israel, preaching peace by Jesus Christ: (he is Lord of all:) That word, I say, ye know, which was published throughout all Judaea, and began from Galilee, after the baptism which John preached; How God anointed Jesus of Nazareth with the Holy Ghost and with power: who went about doing good, and healing all that were oppressed of the devil; for God was with him."* Finally, in Mark 10:43-45 we read the following: *"But so shall it not be among you: but whosoever will be great among you, shall be your minister: And whosoever of you will be the chiefest, shall be servant of all. For even the Son of man came not to be ministered unto, but to minister, and to give his life a ransom for many."*

We know God loves us so much that He sent His Son Jesus into the world to save us from our sins. However, while on this earth, and until His death on the cross, Jesus lived His life serving others. Even though His service often included some type of miracle, we can still follow His example in the way we serve one another today. Please allow me to illustrate this for you by sharing some of the events from the fifth chapter of the book of Mark. In verses one through twenty, we find the account of Jesus casting a legion of demons out of the maniac of Gadara. Being controlled by Satan is nothing new, and we do live in a day when more and more are finding themselves slaves to his vices. Helping those who are enslaved by addictions is truly an act of service. Numerous selfless acts will be needed to bring someone who was once bound by addictions into a life of freedom. An act of service may be as simple as providing a ride to church services, or to necessary meetings which give biblical answers for the problem of addictions, or as practical as giving advice on personal hygiene. We may be called upon to assist in the search for employment, housing, or any number of other areas where we may have some experience.

Along with this story in Chapter 5, we find two others that are linked together. In verse 22, Jairus, a ruler of the synagogue, fell down at Jesus' feet and begged Him to heal his 12-year-old daughter who was at the point of death. While on His way to heal this child, Jesus was interrupted by a woman with a serious physical need. As He cared for her need, news arrived that the young girl had died. Of course, this new development was not a problem for Jesus, and He proceeded to Jairus' home to bring the young girl back to life.

It is heart-rending to me to hear about children who are struggling with a critical illness. When we hear about these types of trials, our act of service could be as simple, yet as powerful, as stopping and taking the time to pray for these young ones and their parents. Even when a child is not critically ill, there may be many other needs. A loss of income may occur at a time of added medical expenses. Also, caring for a sick child can be exhausting for parents who may not be sleeping well. Our act of service could be that of offering a few hours of babysitting so the parents can get some extra rest or run necessary errands. Perhaps our service could be offering to drive family members to doctor appointments, allowing a tired parent to sit with and comfort the sick child. As we look upon these families and see their needs, may we, too, be moved with compassion to be a help in their time of need.

I have a friend who defines compassion as "available action." I wonder if the woman who desired Jesus' help had anyone who was available to help her in her twelve-year sickness. Many years ago, I heard a statement regarding the unexpected events that come into our lives. It was a simple reminder that our interruptions are God's appointments. We can learn much by Jesus' example in how He handled this interruption. He could have spoken harshly to the woman for interrupting Him on His way to help a critically ill, young child, but He did not. Her sickness may not have been critical, but it was important enough to Jesus to stop and help her. It is fairly easy to offer an act of service to someone who is dealing with a two-week illness, but when that illness goes on for an extended period of time, we often fail to see the needs that also continue. Our act of service in this case may be as simple as regularly sending a card with a reminder of our continued prayers. It could be as complex as accompanying the sick one to medical appointments to assist them in understanding the diagnosis and/or treatments, doing additional research, and then communicating that information to other family members.

Several times in the Gospels, we find Jesus being *"moved with compassion."* One of those times is mentioned in Mark Chapter 6, where we find the famous story of the feeding of the five thousand. It really was not Jesus' problem the multitude failed to bring something to eat that day, but He had compassion and provided a meal for all of them. Sharing a meal with those in need is an easy act of service. It could be as effortless as preparing a little extra so there is plenty to share with a widow or widower, or it could be as demanding as preparing a full meal for planned dinner guests.

Lamentations 3:51 says, *"Mine eye affecteth mine heart..."* A great way to "affect one's heart" is to take a short-term mission trip or get to know the missionaries our churches support and become familiar with the conditions under which they serve. This can help us gain a realistic view of how the rest of the world lives. Thankfully, we live in a country with many resources for the poor and their children, but around the world it is not so. It takes very little effort on our part to send funds to various mission organizations so hungry children can be fed both physically and spiritually. Jesus used His acts of service to introduce the lost to the love of God. We must ask ourselves: do

I desire to be full of good deeds, so that I, too, may be used to point others to the love of God?

1. How does God describe Tabitha in Acts 9:36-41?

2. What does He say about her physical appearance?

3. How does God describe Phebe in Romans 16:1-2?

4. What does He say about her physical appearance?

Have you ever stopped to notice how we describe one another? Here are a few descriptions that are actually quite funny: "She is drop-dead gorgeous!" Really? Have you ever seen anyone drop dead? If you have, I am quite certain it was anything but gorgeous. "She is easy on the eyes." Okay, so do you know anyone who is hard on the eyes? I am aware that one could explain these statements to me, but they really do not make much sense at all. We have all given compliments similar to the following: "Her eyes are just beautiful." "Somehow she has maintained her girlish figure." "Her long, thick hair is absolutely gorgeous." "Her make-up is perfect." I am not advocating we cease from giving any compliments about another's physical appearance; however, I would like to submit a thought for you to consider. I wonder what affect it would have on the young ones listening to us if we would describe our friends the way God chose to describe the women we have studied this week. I also wonder what affect it would have on the one being complimented. Surely you would love to hear one of the following statements said about you. "She is the kindest person you will ever meet." "When she gives you her word, you can count on her to come through." "Her words are always so gracious and edifying." "She has an uncanny ability to know just what to say when someone is hurting." "Her knowledge of the Word of God is amazing." "She is full of wisdom from her time in God's Word." "Her love for the Lord is so evident in her service for Him." "She really has a love for those who are hard to love." "She has an amazing spirit, especially when you consider the trials she has faced." "She has a servant's heart." "You will not find anyone who works harder than she does."

Is it possible that our descriptions of one another actually reveal the true desires of our hearts? Instead of focusing on those character qualities that are important to God, so often we are drawn to temporal qualities. Why is that? What was the enemy to the Psalmist's desire when he said, *"I shall be satisfied when I awake with thy likeness?"* That is a question I hope to answer for you next week as we study the subject of our greatest enemy.

Week Four

Our Greatest Enemy

Something to Think About

At my one-year post-operative appointment, the reality of what my future could possibly look like was becoming more clear. My surgeon explained to me how the nerves in the upper third part of the face are always the most difficult to awaken, and in many cases they never do. The muscles, in their paralyzed condition, cause my right eyebrow and lid to droop, making it impossible to apply eye make-up to my right eye. This also causes my glasses to appear to rest at an odd angle on my face. My surgeon did, however, offer me some encouragement regarding the Synkinesis when he referred me to an occupational therapist in the Denver area. He explained to me that she had seen some success in treating her patients who had symptoms similar to mine. I made an appointment with her, and she made it clear to me the process of breaking up the mis-wired facial nerves could take two to three years. However, she felt the bad connection could be corrected. As we met together, I was shocked to learn the exercises I had been doing for the past nine months were actually hurting my condition rather than helping it. I was disappointed by this revelation, but I hoped it would help my physical therapist see the need for further training regarding the treatment of facial muscle paralysis.

My next scheduled appointment was with my eye doctor to determine if my cornea had healed sufficiently in order for me to once again wear contact lenses. When the exam was completed, she felt like I was indeed ready. The contacts were ordered, and a one-month trial period began. I had been wearing mono-vision contact lenses for many years prior to my surgery. Since I am left-eye dominant, the lens for my left eye is my distance lens, and the lens for my right eye is my reading lens. I followed the directions for my new lenses carefully hoping each day would bring more clarity to my right eye. I had, however, been warned by another doctor not to get my hopes up. She explained that wearing mono-vision lenses can sometimes be too taxing on the brain after a brain trauma. I had never had any issues with them in the past, but after the trial period, I simply could not see clearly enough to read with my right eye. We decided to wait an additional year to see if further healing would enable my brain to tolerate the use of the new lenses.

Prior to my surgery, I asked to be anointed with oil, specifically addressing some of the issues with which I am now living. The Apostle Paul asked for the healing of his *"thorn in the flesh,"* and God's answer was *"...My grace is sufficient for thee: for my strength is made perfect in weakness..."* (2 Cor. 12:9). I asked to be anointed because the Lord instructs us to ask in James 5:13-15: *"Is any among you afflicted? let him pray. Is any merry? let him sing psalms. Is any sick among you? let him call for the elders of the church; and let them pray over him, anointing him with oil in the name of the Lord: And the prayer of faith shall save the sick, and the Lord shall raise him up; and if he have committed sins, they shall be forgiven him."* In His darkest hour, Jesus asked His Father to remove the suffering He was about to face, but even in asking He submitted to the will of His Heavenly Father when He said, *"... if thou be willing, remove this cup from me: nevertheless not my will, but thine, be done"* (Luke 22:42).

As I went into surgery, my heart was humbled before the Father. I believe this is why He gave me the grace to accept the things that happened as a result of the tumor being deeper and harder to remove than expected. However, that post-surgical grace did not last past my initial state of humility. Each time I find myself in a discontented state, I must humble myself anew to find His grace once again sufficient. *"For we have not an high priest which cannot be touched with the feeling of our infirmities; but was in all points tempted like as we are, yet without sin. Let us therefore come boldly unto the throne of grace, that we may obtain mercy, and find grace to help in time of need"* (Heb. 4:15-16).

Grace, the power of God to accomplish the will of God, is a specific by-product of humility. In James 4:6, we are told: *"...God resisteth the proud, but giveth grace unto the humble."* Then in 1 Peter 5:5 we read: *"...Yea, all of you be subject one to another, and be clothed with humility: for God resisteth the proud, and giveth grace to the humble."* In Luke 1:38, we find the mother of Jesus humbling herself before the angel Gabriel as she makes the following statement: *"...Behold the handmaid of the Lord; be it unto me according to thy word..."* Her appearance and life were about to drastically change. Not only would she be unable to hide the baby growing in her womb, but she would bear the reproach of His conception throughout her lifetime.

In our pride, we can find ourselves thinking, "God, I know you can do better than this; just look at how beautiful you created my sister." His words gently remind us: *"For we dare not make ourselves of the number, or compare ourselves with some that commend themselves; but they measuring themselves by themselves, and comparing themselves along themselves, are not wise"* (2 Cor. 10:12). In our pride we admit, "Lord, just once, I wish I could be the one everyone considers pretty." He speaks truth to our hearts with: *"For we commend not ourselves again unto you, but give you occasion to glory on our behalf, that ye may have somewhat to answer them which glory in appearance, and not in heart"* (2 Cor. 5:12). When in our pride we declare some physical feature that we hate, He makes it perfectly clear, *"Nay but, O man, who art thou that repliest against God? Shall the thing formed say to him that formed it, Why hast thou made me thus? Hath not the potter power over the clay, of the same lump to make one vessel unto honour, and another unto dishonour"* (Rom. 9:20-21)?

I would like to be able to tell you that Hollywood is our greatest enemy in this matter of accepting the appearance God has given us, or has allowed to be altered, but that is not true. Our greatest enemy is our own pride. This week we will look closely at this enemy we fight on a daily basis. In so doing, I pray we will not only become better equipped to recognize our enemy, but also gain the victory over him.

The *American Dictionary of the English Language* by Noah Webster 1828 defines the word "pride" as the following: "Inordinate self-esteem; an unreasonable conceit of one's own superiority in talents, beauty, wealth, accomplishments, rank or elevation in office, which manifests itself in lofty airs, distance, reserve, and often in contempt of others." Although I prefer to use the Greek or Hebrew definitions, I believe Mr. Webster's definition is very applicable to our study this week.

As we begin, we must first understand where pride originates. In Isaiah Chapter 14, verses 12 through 14 we read: *"How art thou fallen from heaven, O Lucifer, son of the morning! how art thou cut down to the ground, which didst weaken the nations! For thou hast said in thine heart, I will ascend into heaven, I will exalt my throne above the stars of God: I will sit also upon the mount of the congregation, in the sides of the north: I will ascend above the heights of the clouds; I will be like the most High."* Please notice these were not Lucifer's words, but rather his thoughts. These verses give us a very clear picture of the destruction that comes to one whose heart or mind is filled with pride. We simply cannot hide our thoughts from God.

It should not surprise us when God warns that any real change must first be made in our minds. *"I beseech you therefore, brethren, by the mercies of God, that ye present your bodies a living sacrifice, holy, acceptable unto God, which is your reasonable service. And be not conformed to this world: but be ye transformed by the renewing of your mind, that ye may prove what is that good, and acceptable, and perfect, will of God. For I say, through the grace given unto me, to every man that is among you, not to think of himself more highly than he ought to think; but to think soberly, according as God hath dealt to every man the measure of faith"* (Rom. 12:1-3). The remaining verses in this chapter give us instructions for using our various gifts in the local body of believers, the correct treatment of one another, and concludes by giving the purpose for this behavior - that of overcoming evil with good. My thinking about my appearance, or any other area of my life, is not something that affects me alone; it affects every area of my life. Therefore, if I am to be used of God to overcome evil with good, I must recognize those areas in which I think of myself more highly, or more often, than I ought to think.

In Ezekiel 28:14-17 we read the following: *"Thou art the anointed cherub that covereth; and I have set thee so: thou wast upon the holy mountain of God; thou hast walked up and down in the midst of the stones of fire. Thou wast perfect in thy ways from the day that thou wast created, till iniquity was found in thee. By the multitude of thy merchandise they have filled the midst of thee with violence, and thou hast sinned: therefore I will cast thee as profane out of the mountain of God: and I will destroy thee, O covering cherub, from the midst of the stones of fire. Thine heart was lifted up because of thy beauty, thou hast corrupted thy wisdom by reason of thy brightness: I will cast thee to the ground, I will lay thee before kings, that they may behold thee."* There are some differences of opinions by Bible scholars as to whether or not this is a reference to Satan or to a Historical king, but we need not decide which opinion we hold for our purposes here. The fact of the matter is this creation of God had a heart full of pride because of the very beauty given by God. Oh, that each of us would see any good thing about our creation as a gift from God, for His Word has made it clear that *"... in me (that is, in my flesh,) dwelleth no good thing: for to will is present with me; but how to perform that which is good I find not"* (Rom. 7:18).

Pride exalts oneself to be equal with God; humility lowers oneself in submission to God. There are many comparisons of these two attitudes in the Word of God. Today we are going to take some time to examine some of them. Read each of the following Scripture passages, and, in your own words, compare the results of both pride and humility.

1. Proverbs 11:2

2. Proverbs 16:18-19

3. Proverbs 29:23

4. Matthew 23:11-12

5. Philippians 2:1-8

6. 1 Peter 5:5-6

Today in our study, we will look at pride and how it relates to our position. Many years ago, I was caring for the children of some of the women in our church while they were making visits to the unchurched people in our area. The pure humor provided by children is my favorite kind of humor, so, just for fun, I decided to ask them what they wanted to be when they grew up and why. One of the little girls responded by saying, "I want to be a pastor's wife, so I can tell everybody what to do." I was horrified; yet her simple, honest answer provoked me to do some deep soul-searching.

As a pastor's wife, it is my responsibility to meet the personal needs of the pastor. My responsibilities are no different than the electrician's wife, the plumber's wife, the teacher's wife, the executive's wife, et al. As a mother, it is my responsibility to meet the needs of our children and to train them in the ways of the Lord. *"And these words, which I command thee this day, shall be in thine heart: And thou shalt teach them diligently unto thy children, and shalt talk of them when thou sittest in thine house, and when thou walkest by the way, and when thou liest down, and when thou risest up"* (Deut. 6:6-7). As a Christian, it is my responsibility to love God and to love others in obedience to His commandments. *"And Jesus answered him, The first of all the commandments is, Hear, O Israel; The Lord our God is one Lord: And thou shalt love the Lord thy God with all thy heart, and with all thy soul, and with all thy mind, and with all thy strength: this is the first commandment. And the second is like, namely this, Thou shalt love thy neighbour as thyself. There is none other commandment greater than these"* (Mark 12:29-31). Whatever position God gives me as I live this Christian life is simply an opportunity to serve others and, in turn, influence them to desire to serve the Lord. Pride sets in when we put more emphasis on our position than in the One Who placed us there. We are told in Psalm 75:6-7, *"...promotion cometh neither from the east, nor from the west, nor from the south. But God is the judge: he putteth down one, and setteth up another."* Today, we are going to look at a lady to whom God gave great influence through her position, but, in the end, succumbed to pride and forfeited her opportunity to influence others.

We are first introduced to Miriam in Exodus Chapter 2 when we find her watching over her baby brother Moses. *"And when she could not longer hide him, she took for him an ark of bulrushes, and daubed it with slime and with pitch, and put the child therein; and she laid it in the flags by the river's brink. And his sister stood afar off, to wit what would be done to him. And the daughter of Pharaoh came down to wash herself at the river; and her maidens walked along by the river's side; and when she saw the ark among the flags, she sent her maid to fetch it. And when she had opened it, she saw the child: and, behold, the babe wept. And she had compassion on him, and said, This is one of the Hebrews' children. Then said his sister to Pharaoh's daughter, Shall I go and call to thee a nurse of the Hebrew women, that she may nurse the child for thee? And Pharaoh's daughter said to her, Go. And the maid went and called the child's mother"* (Ex. 2:3-8).

Miriam showed great responsibility and maturity in how she watched over Moses and handled herself with Pharaoh's daughter. The next time we hear of her, she has been given the title of "prophetess," the chief singer to her brother, Aaron, the priest. In her new position, she showed great leadership as she led the women in a song proclaiming the great things God had just done for the children of Israel. *"And Miriam the prophetess, the sister of Aaron, took a timbrel in her hand; and all the women went out after her with timbrels and with dances. And Miriam answered them, Sing ye to the LORD, for he hath triumphed gloriously; the horse and his rider hath he thrown into the sea"* (Ex. 15:20-21).

Then something happened deep within Miriam's heart. Read Numbers 12:1-15, and answer the questions below:

1. Who stood up for Moses when his brother and sister complained to him regarding his authority?

2. What happened to Miriam as a result of her prideful rebellion?

3. Who stood up for Miriam?

After this incident, we no longer hear of Miriam being used of God in a place of leadership. It is wonderful to realize that God chose Miriam for a prominent place of leadership without any mention of her physical appearance because our physical beauty, or lack thereof, has nothing to do with how God can use us as we humble ourselves before Him. When we refuse to be content with the position God has given us, whether great or small, we lose the influence He has designed for us to have in that position.

Before concluding today, I would like us to briefly look at another lady who held a prominent position. Jezebel was the daughter of King Ethbaal, who was the king of the Zidonians, and also the priest of Baal worshippers. She brought this worship into her marriage with King Ahab. She was a strong woman who used her strength to be an influence for evil rather than for good. Read 1 Kings Chapter 21, and answer the questions below:

4. In verse 25 of this chapter, the Bible tells us there was no one like Ahab in his work of wickedness; however, it also tells us Jezebel was the one who stirred him up. The definition of "stirred up" means to "incite, allure, instigate, or entice." What position of leadership do you currently hold, and are you using your position to inspire godliness or to incite evil?

5. What promise did God give to Ahab in verse 29, and why did God give him this promise?

Today in our study, we will look at pride and how it relates to our possessions. I spent my early childhood years living in a three-story, brick duplex in inner city Harrisburg, Pennsylvania. The neighborhood children loved running and jumping over the brick barrier between the two homes and catching fireflies in the front yard while our parents and neighbors sat on their front porches watching us. Our kitchen walls, made of bare plaster, were stained with the flood waters from the Susquehanna River. My three siblings and I loved measuring ourselves and looking forward to the day when we would be as tall as the flood line. My two sisters and I shared a bedroom that had walls covered with old, dark pink wallpaper, onto which we would sometimes carve pictures using our fingernails, or write out our latest frustrations. Our bedroom had a staircase that led to the attic where we would explore old treasures when the heat was not too stifling to allow us to do so.

My father had grown up in the inner city, and it was his dream to build a home on some acreage, which he did when I became a teenager. It was just a simple ranch style home, but he was so happy to be out of the city. During the process of building our new home, my mother was diagnosed with breast cancer. I remember shopping with my dad for a cherry wood dining room table, chairs, and hutch to surprise her. Sadly, she did not get to enjoy them, nor our new home on seven acres for very long. She passed away in 1974 at the age of 42. She was a real buddy to my father, and because of her sacrifices, he was able to be self-employed running a business that would often take him away from us for several days at a time. However, when he was in town, he spent time with his family, whether that meant we were all working with him in our basement, or fishing with him on a lake.

My father was a very giving man. When he sold tapestries, my visiting girlfriends went home with a tapestry; when he sold luggage, my visiting girlfriends went home with a new piece of luggage. Best of all, when he sold jewelry, my visiting girlfriends went home with a new piece of jewelry. He was very fond of the verse in Matthew 6:3: *"But when thou doest alms, let not thy left hand know what thy right hand doeth."* He firmly believed we should give to others without fanfare, and that is exactly what he did. I do not remember ever feeling as though life was about gaining possessions, but rather sharing them. I am sure God also used the premature death of my mother to instill in me an appreciation for the things that really matter in this life, which are the relationships we can take with us to Heaven.

In Luke Chapter 12, beginning in verse 16, we read the parable of the rich man who, because of his increased goods, felt the necessity to build bigger buildings to contain them. Then in verses 19-21 we read: *"And I will say to my soul, Soul, thou hast much goods laid up for many years; take thine ease, eat, drink, and be merry. But God said unto him, Thou fool, this night thy soul shall be required of thee: then whose shall those things be, which thou hast provided? So is he that layeth up treasure for himself, and is not rich toward God."* This passage goes on to tell us we should not worry about what we will eat, and drink, or what we will wear. It is a parallel passage to Matthew 6:25-34 where we have the famous verse 33: *"But seek ye first the kingdom of God, and his righteousness; and all these things shall be added unto you."* In verses 19-21 of Matthew 6 we read: *"Lay not up for yourselves treasures upon earth, where moth and rust doth corrupt, and where thieves break through and steal: But lay up for yourselves treasures in heaven, where neither moth nor rust doth corrupt, and where thieves do not break through nor steal: For where your treasure is, there will your heart be also."*

As I read the story of this rich man, I could not help but wonder if he had a wife or girlfriend who placed too much importance on worldly possessions. Rather than building a larger home to contain our possessions, perhaps it would be a good practice to give a portion of our abundance to others. When our closets are full, it may be time to pull out those things we rarely use and pass them on to someone in need. When our floor space is full, it may be time to pass on some of those belongings to others in need. Finding difficulty in letting go of things is nothing new. In Luke 17:28-32 we read: *"Likewise also as it was in the days of Lot; they did eat, they drank, they bought, they sold, they planted, they builded; But the same day that Lot went out of Sodom it rained fire and brimstone from heaven, and destroyed them all. Even thus shall it be in the day when the Son of man is revealed. In that day, he which shall be upon the housetop, and his stuff in the house, let him not come down to take it away: and he that is in the field, let him likewise not return back. Remember Lot's wife."* Let us do as verse 32 admonishes and *"remember Lot's wife."*

Read Genesis 19:12-26, and answer the questions below:

1. How many of Lot's friends and family members were saved from this tragedy?

2. If you had been in this family, what might have been your reason for lingering?

3. Is there anything you own for which you would risk one last glimpse?

In Acts 4:34-5:10, we read about a time in history when many of the believers practiced selflessness and sacrifice. They were not required by the church to sell their possessions, nor were they required to bring any particular amount to the church. However, there was a man named Barnabas who did receive praise for his self-sacrifice. Read the Scripture passage noted above, and answer the questions below:

4. What possible motive could have led to the deception of Ananias and Sapphira?

5. What is the underlying reason for these motives?

Several years ago, our good friend, Randy Casey, made a statement I will never forget. He said, "Junk is the stuff we throw away, and stuff is the junk we keep." Each and every one of our possessions is given to us by the Lord. We must be willing to use them in service for the Lord instead of hoarding them for our own selfish purposes.

Today in our study, we will look at pride and how it relates to what we do for pleasure. We often refer to Sunday as the Lord's Day; however, the truth is every day is the Lord's Day. Even though there are several days each week in which we labor to provide for our families and for others, these days still belong to the Lord, and hopefully we labor as unto the Lord. Of course, I recognize our work does not cease at the end of our paid "work day." The Lord expects us to be good stewards of all He has given us. Part of the responsibility of being a good steward is to work at keeping our bodies, our homes, our vehicles, our clothing, etc., in good condition, so they may be used for God's honor and glory. There is also a day, or a few days each month, we refer to as "my day off," but is it really "my day?" In 1 Corinthians 10:31, the Apostle Paul writes: *"Whether therefore ye eat, or drink, or whatsoever ye do, do all to the glory of God."* Colossians 3:17 further explains: *"And whatsoever ye do in word or deed, do all in the name of the Lord Jesus, giving thanks to God and the Father by him."* Then just a few verses later in this chapter we are told: *"And whatsoever ye do, do it heartily, as to the Lord, and not unto men"* (vs. 23). Our days, whether they be the "Lord's Day," our work days, or our day(s) off, are given to us to use to bring honor and glory to God.

Several times in the Gospels, we find Jesus heading up into the mountains, or out into the wilderness. His purpose for doing so was to spend time alone with His Heavenly Father. What we choose to do for pleasure should be done with His purpose in mind. That purpose may be as simple as setting aside extra time to spend in Bible study and prayer, or it may be as complex as making extra time to invest in the lives of our family and others.

Many years ago, a middle-aged woman began attending our church and approached me about the possibility of us doing some hiking together. At the time, our youngest son had not yet fulfilled his homeschool requirement for physical education, so we included him on our hikes. This woman felt "at home" in the outdoors, and hiking provided her with an environment where she felt very comfortable asking me a ton of questions regarding the Christian life. In appreciation for giving her my time, she provided me with the training and gear needed to do some high-altitude hiking. In August of 2004 at the age of 47, I climbed Mt. Belford, my first fourteen-thousand-foot mountain (fourteener) with our two youngest sons. It was the most difficult physical activity in which I had ever participated, but God taught me so much through that challenge. Not only was it one of the most precious memories I have with Dave and Jack, but it was a catalyst for how God would use this activity to allow me to minister to others.

Since that day, I have completed 31 climbs on 15 different fourteeners. I would like to point out that I live at an elevation of eight-thousand, five-hundred feet, and the trails for these climbs all started between ten and twelve-thousand feet. These types of "climbs" are not technical in nature and do not require the use of ropes; however, they are very strenuous, uphill hikes, with a distance of two to seven miles to reach the summit. While I would never say these hikes are easy, I also do not want to make them sound more dramatic than they actually are. I have been privileged to climb with seven different adults and 19 different young people.

In this environment where the young people felt comfortable, I would often begin the hike by asking them to look for the lessons God would have for us on the climb. Over the years, God taught us many lessons from His book of nature, and I would like to share just a few of them. On my first attempt to climb Colorado's highest peak, a lightning storm moved in and forced us back down just before reaching the summit. One of the young people boldly proclaimed, "I'll tell you what God was teaching us today; if you hang around sin too long you are going to get fried, just like we almost did by not getting off the mountain sooner!" On a different hike, a young person surprised me when he said, "Mrs. Parton, I want to tell you about the time when God showed me my pride." I could tell you about the female athlete whose main goal was to get up and down the mountain in record time. It has been such a joy to watch her mature over the years as she has learned to enjoy the journey as much as the accomplishment. One young man in particular has accompanied me on one-third of my climbs, often because his mother did not want him to climb without me. I found this rather humorous because that young man was far more experienced than I was. He is now married, and I hope he is a better husband because of his experiences climbing the mountains with a woman old enough to be his mother! He learned to remain kind in spite of my slow pace, to remain patient as I took many photos, and to look out for my needs on the trail.

I did not always climb with the intention of teaching the young people; sometimes I climbed with a need in my own heart to draw closer to the Lord. I wish there was enough space to share the many lessons God taught me and the ways in which He has shown Himself to me, but I am thankful for a friend who introduced me to an avenue where I could learn to know Him better.

We have already learned that God has given each of us various talents and abilities which we can use to simply enjoy all He has for us. As we make plans for "our days off," may we humbly seek what He would want even in our times of pleasure.

1. Read 1 Timothy 5:1-15. What was Paul's concern about young widows and their time of leisure?

2. Read Titus 2:3-5. What principles are older women commanded to teach to younger women?

3. What do you enjoy doing for pleasure?

4. How are you using, or how can you use, this activity to bring glory to God?

Today in our study, we will look at pride and how it relates to our popularity. Noah Webster's 1828 Dictionary states the definition of the word "popularity" as "Favor of the people; the state of possessing the affections and confidence of the people in general." God's timing is always perfect, and I should not continue to be amazed by it; however, in this lesson it was particularly heart felt. I "just happened" to be studying this principle as our four Colorado grandchildren, along with their parents, were preparing to move to New Mexico. Our other three children live in close proximity to their spouse's parents. Although our Colorado grandchildren lived three hours away, it still allowed us to see them multiple times a year. I remember that my Nana was my favorite grandparent simply because she was there for us every school day. She would take the city bus to our home and arrive just before we left for school. Each day when we arrived home from school, she was there to help us with our homework and play board games. I did not dislike my other grandparents; I just did not know them as well.

When our first grandchild was born, I made the decision that I would not compete with the other grandparents; however, I have found living with that decision has not always been easy. I have to constantly re-train my mind to be grateful for the other grandparents and pray for their investment in the lives of our grandchildren. I must discipline my mind to trust the Lord and the place He has chosen for me in the lives of our grandchildren, even if that place is separated by many miles.

One of the main desires in the Apostle Paul's life was for the gospel to be preached. In Philippians 1:12-18 we read the following: *"But I would ye should understand, brethren, that the things which happened unto me have fallen out rather unto the furtherance of the gospel; So that my bonds in Christ are manifest in all the palace, and in all other places; And many of the brethren in the Lord, waxing confident by my bonds, are much more bold to speak the word without fear. Some indeed preach Christ even of envy and strife; and some also of good will: The one preach Christ of contention, not sincerely, supposing to add affliction to my bonds: But the other of love, knowing that I am set for the defence of the gospel. What then? notwithstanding, every way, whether in pretence, or in truth, Christ is preached; and I therein do rejoice, yea, and will rejoice."* Paul's imprisonment caused many believers to become emboldened to fearlessly preach the Word of God. However, there were also those who were jealous of Paul and preached the Word of God with wrong motives. The word "contention" in verse 16 speaks of a rivalry and is self-seeking. Sadly, these men were preaching to promote themselves rather than to see souls saved. Oh, how I desire to be used of God to encourage our grandchildren to place their trust in Him and then to love Him with all their hearts, souls, minds, and strength. However, if I do so with a desire of promoting myself over the other grandparents, I am sinning and failing to fulfill God's purpose for me in their lives.

Favoritism is nothing new, and, in the 29th Chapter of Genesis, the Lord gives us an example of its consequences. Here are just a few excerpts from that story: *"And Laban had two daughters: the name of the elder was Leah, and the name of the younger was Rachel. Leah was tender eyed; but Rachel was beautiful and well favoured. And Jacob loved Rachel; and said, I will serve thee seven years for Rachel thy younger daughter… and he loved also Rachel more than Leah, and served with him yet seven other years. And when the LORD saw that Leah was hated, he opened her womb: but Rachel was barren."* We see that Jacob specifically favored Rachel over Leah because of her beauty; however, Rachel's popularity did not stop the Lord from seeing Leah's plight, nor from doing something to be an encouragement to her. Just a few chapters later, we find Jacob showing favoritism to Rachel's firstborn son, Joseph.

Joseph and his brother Benjamin were Jacob's youngest sons, the only sons of his beloved wife, Rachel. The favoritism shown to Joseph was a breeding ground for his brothers' jealousy. Even though their sin made Joseph's life miserable, he chose not to allow it to ruin his life. He continued to trust God in his trials and faithfully served Him. God then gave Joseph favor in the eyes of his Egyptian captors which eventually allowed him to save the lives of his entire family during the widespread famine.

Not only is this story a warning to us if we desire to be "the favored one," but it can also give us instruction on how to respond if we find ourselves in that position. Luke 2:52 tells us that Jesus, "... *increased in wisdom and stature, and in favour with God and man.*" May we first and foremost seek to find favor with God and trust Him, whether or not we find favor with man.

Read the verses below, and answer the questions making note of the change that came to Leah's heart.

1. According to Genesis 29:32, what did Leah hope the birth of her son, Reuben, would do?

2. According to Genesis 29:33, why did Leah believe God gave her a second son named Simeon?

3. According to Genesis 29:34, what did Leah hope the birth of her son, Levi, would do?

4. According to Genesis 29:35, what was Leah's reaction to the birth of her fourth son, Judah?

I was pleasantly surprised to read about the transformation that came to Leah's heart as her desires changed from seeking to gain Jacob's favor to simply praising the Lord for His goodness to her. Did you see yourself in the life of this woman? My sister and I have often joked about which one of us was our mother, or father's favorite. I cannot tell you how many times I tried to earn my mother's favor during our childhood, or how often I felt jealousy toward my sister. Thankfully, our friendship overcame the sting of hurt we felt because of the favoritism. I cannot go back and relive those years, but I can choose not to make the same mistake in the lives of our grandchildren. I want each of them to feel as though he/she is my favorite, and I must not allow myself to wonder whether, or not, I am theirs.

Are you seeking to gain popularity in the life of someone? Will you choose to humble yourself before the Lord, trusting Him with the place He has for you to occupy in that life?

Today in our study, we will look at pride and how it relates to our priorities. Each morning as we open our eyes and climb out of bed, we have a decision to make. Do we make the bed immediately, save it for later, or wait until we crawl back in at the end of the day? This decision will depend upon our priorities. If you are the young mother who was awakened at 5 a.m. by a hungry infant, the making of your bed may need to wait. If you also have a sick two-year-old, it may need to wait even longer. Just for fun, add a five-year-old sister who must eat a nutritious meal before going off to school. Between cleaning up after the two-year-old, caring for your infant, and making sure the five-year-old gets to school on time, you may not see your bed again until that glorious time of day we refer to as "nap time." However, what if you add a seven-year-old brother to the mix, and you are a homeschooling mom? Once you care for your infant, clean up after your sick two-year-old, teach the five-year-old her newest phonics blends, and help the seven-year-old recite his multiplication tables, you may not even see your bed again until everyone has settled in for the night. This does not mean making your bed is unimportant; it simply means it is less important than the four little people the Lord has given you to rear for His honor and glory. It is our pride that longs for some peace and quiet to do what we want to do. We may be tempted to close our bedroom door to all of those needs rather than humble ourselves to meet them, but motherhood can only be done successfully if it is done selflessly.

If you are reading this book, you are no doubt someone who believes in the importance of growing your relationship with God through the Word of God. Perhaps you are the lady who turns off your alarm, turns on your light, and snuggles up to the Word of God first thing each morning. Perhaps you have to wake up first with a shower before choosing to sit down with your cup of coffee and your Bible. Maybe you take it one step further by first getting some food in your stomach so you can think clearly as you read God's Word. If you are the young mother mentioned in the paragraph above, you may be looking forward to any small window in your day when you can sit down with your Bible, even if that window does not come until all of the little ones are tucked into bed for what you hope will be a good night's sleep. We are not commanded in the Word of God to read our Bibles at any particular time of day, nor are we given any command regarding how much we are to read. However, we are commanded to *"Study to shew thyself approved unto God, a workman that needeth not to be ashamed, rightly dividing the word of truth"* (2 Tim. 2:15). We are also given an example to follow in the lives of the people of Berea: *"And the brethren immediately sent away Paul and Silas by night unto Berea: who coming thither went into the synagogue of the Jews. These were more noble than those in Thessalonica, in that they received the word with all readiness of mind, and searched the scriptures daily, whether those things were so"* (Acts 17:10-11). Each of the ladies above may place a priority on getting to know God better through His Word, but the key to their success will be instituting a plan for spending time with the Lord. Benjamin Franklin is famous for many things, but I love his quote: "If you fail to plan, you are planning to fail."

We need to understand our relationship with God is our number one priority; however, God also sees our relationships with one another as a high priority. *"Let nothing be done through strife or vainglory; but in lowliness of mind let each esteem other better than themselves. Look not every man on his own things, but every man also on the things of others"* (Phil. 2:3-4). God's Word instructs us to love one another and that love is to be manifested through many acts of service toward one another.

We have a beautiful example of caring for others in the story of Ruth and Naomi. Elimelech and his wife, Naomi, along with their two sons, Mahlon and Chilion, moved from Judah to the country of Moab, because of a severe famine. Sadly, Elimelech died shortly after their arrival leaving Naomi a widow. After his death, the two sons married Moabite young ladies and settled into married life when tragedy struck this family again. Both sons died leaving Naomi with two widowed daughters-in-law. Broken and bitter, she decided to return to Judah and encouraged the girls to return to their father's houses.

Read Ruth 1:11-2:23, and answer the questions below:

1. What was Ruth's answer to Naomi's encouragement for her to go home?

2. How did Ruth humbly choose to serve Naomi?

3. What was it about Ruth that caught the eye of Boaz?

4. If you have ever done any harvesting, you know it is hard, dirty work. In the third verse of Chapter 3, what did Naomi instruct Ruth to do before she approached Boaz about the possibility of being her kinsman redeemer?

5. Read Ruth 4:13-22, and list the blessings both Ruth and Naomi received as a result of Ruth choosing to put the needs of her mother-in-law above her own?

Many years ago, my husband was a camp director where teenagers volunteered as counselors and other camp workers. He would instruct the young ladies to "fix up in the morning, then forget about yourselves, and focus on the children." We must always remember our ministry to others is of greater importance than our appearance. How we "fix up" should not be done with the goal of drawing attention to ourselves, but rather something we should do in order to better care for those around us. Imagine the reaction we would get if we delivered a meal in an outfit that had been splattered with the meal we just prepared. This would not be very appealing! Dropping by to visit a neighbor when our breath smells like a dirty sock is not very welcoming. Volunteering to help at the church when our hair has not been washed in a week and the dirty laundry is piled high at home, may not be an appropriate application of our priorities. As we head into the final weeks of this study, we will begin to look more specifically at this matter of our physical appearance and its proper place in our lives.

Week Five

Beauty Comes with a Warning Label

Something to Think About

Later this week, we will address some warnings that are mentioned in the Word of God regarding potential pitfalls of physical beauty, but first I must lay some important ground-work for heeding those warnings. As I write, I am 18 months into my recovery, and I am currently seeking the Lord for His direction in what to do about my hearing loss due to my deaf right ear. At the present time, we know of two options, and neither of them will have much impact upon my appearance. In a quiet environment, when speaking one-on-one I can hear just fine; however, when I am in a public place, hearing is difficult due to all of the background noise. We live in a noisy world, and, once again, I am reminded of the necessity of taking time to be still and quiet before the Lord.

Last week I mentioned some of the lessons learned while climbing the mountains near our home in Colorado. I would like to share another example as an introduction to this week's topic. One of the young ladies in our church, who was preparing to go to an out-of-state Bible college, approached me about the possibility of taking her on a trek up one of our fourteeners. This was the first time I led a climb, so I was extremely astute about our surroundings. The trail we chose was a "class two" trail, meaning the trail would require us to do some scrambling between rocks and use our hands from time to time. However, one of the most distinct characteristics of a "class two" trail is that sections of the trail seem to simply disappear making it necessary to look for and follow "cairns" - piles of rocks left by previous hikers to mark the way. There are sections of the trail above the tree line where there is nothing but rock making it very difficult to see the cairns. When this is the case, it is necessary to frequently stop and look for the next marker before proceeding forward. If a hiker makes a decision not to follow the cairns, he can find himself in great danger. Sadly, when we hear of tragedies in the mountains, it is often because someone failed to prepare, or failed to follow the guidelines given by those who were more experienced.

As my young friend and I were discussing the gratitude we felt for those who left the cairns, we noticed a buzzing sound. We began searching for what sounded like an electronic device. Imagine our surprise when we noticed the sound was coming from a large bumble bee! We had no idea they could live at such high altitude! Had we been in the city, I doubt we would have even noticed him; however, in the quiet of the mountaintop, his sound was loud and clear. As we discussed this further, we talked about a few of the cairns we each had in our lives. The Word of God has been given to us as a "cairn" to direct our paths. Our parents and leaders have been used of God to give us "cairns" through their instructions on how to live a successful life. How thankful we were for these reminders to stop, look, and listen, so that we might better navigate the life God has given us.

We are admonished in Scripture to "...*hearken unto me, O ye children: for blessed are they that keep my ways*" (Prov. 8:32). The word "hearken" means "to hear, to listen, to give heed, obey," and this is exactly the wise response we should give to any warning. One of the greatest warnings about beauty was given by King Solomon to his young son, Rehoboam, in the book of Proverbs: "*Lust not after her beauty in thine heart; neither let her take thee with her eyelids*" (6:25). "*Lust not*" was a warning not "to desire, delight in, or covet" this young woman's beauty. The passage further warns of the destruction that comes as a result of the sin of adultery. For our purposes, I want to emphasize the context of this warning which is "*My son, keep thy father's commandment, and forsake not the law of thy mother: Bind them continually upon thine heart, and tie them about thy neck. When thou goest, it shall lead thee; when thou sleepest, it shall keep thee; and when thou awakest, it shall talk with thee. For the commandment is a lamp; and the law is light; and reproofs of instruction are the way of life: To keep thee from the evil woman..."* (Prov. 6:20-24a). We have already stated that the instruction of our parents and leaders can be likened to the cairns which guide hikers to the summit of a mountain. In the passage above, we have the record of a father who gave guidance to his son, warning him away from a sin that would lead to a life of destruction. Tomorrow's lesson contains an account of a father who gave guidance to his daughter. It is my desire that we would *"hearken unto"* the examples the Lord has given us so we may be better equipped to help those in our care.

Each of us have grown up with rules and standards set forth by our parents or guardians. When I was growing up, my family and I spent much of our leisure time fishing and swimming. My father had some specific rules regarding the swimsuits my sisters and I were allowed to wear. We were allowed to choose either a one-piece or two-piece suit, as long as our belly button was covered. I remember very vividly standing in line at the dressing room awaiting my turn to try on a new swimsuit. A lady standing in front of me told me I had much too nice of a figure to hide it in the suit I had chosen. In that moment, I had a choice to make: choose to follow the instruction of my father, or secretly choose something more revealing and hide it from him. Fortunately, he had built a close relationship with me, and I wanted to honor him, no matter what this stranger thought. I trusted him when he explained his reasons for the standard he set for me. I am sure the relationship my father and I shared not only kept me from disobeying his wishes many years ago, but actually caused me to strengthen my standards as I got older.

Several years ago, our son, Jon, and I were having a conversation about our relationship with Christ and the standards by which we choose to live. In our conversation Jon made the following statement: "Rules without relationships produce rebellion." In our 40 plus years in ministry, I can truly say I have witnessed this truth in action. If we are going to be used of the Lord to warn the young ladies in our lives about the potential pitfalls of physical beauty, we must first build a relationship with them. We will then have a good foundation on which to guide them in their walk with God. As they grow older, they will need our guidance less and less, but if they have built a relationship with the Lord it is likely they will continue to seek to please Him with the standards by which they choose to live.

We see a beautiful example of this kind of relationship in the life of Mordecai and Esther. We enter their story as the Persian King Ahasuerus, also known as Xerxes, was hosting a feast in which he displayed all of the amazing beauty of his empire. It was a Persian custom at these events to consume alcohol in such quantity that this feast could be classified as a drunken party. Queen Vashti threw a feast of her own during the same time, but hers was interrupted when her drunken husband made an ungodly demand of her. In Esther 1:10-11 we read: *On the seventh day, when the heart of the king was merry with wine, he commanded Mehuman, Biztha, Harbona, Bigtha, and Abagtha, Zethar, and Carcas, the seven chamberlains that served in the presence of Ahasuerus the king, To bring Vashti the queen before the king with the crown royal, to shew the people and the princes her beauty: for she was fair to look on.* The meaning of the word "beauty" used in this passage is "to be beautiful, comely in person, by nature or art; beautiful in action, in wisdom, in season, and in suitableness: it implies beauty internal as well as external." The word "fair" used here means to be "good in a very extensive sense."

Vashti was a good woman, and not knowing what would happen if she were to appear before this group of drunken men, she refused. The king, fearing her actions would set a precedent for other women in his kingdom to disobey their husbands, dethroned Vashti and made a new decree which strengthened the authority given to husbands. Vashti bravely took a stand to protect her own purity, which paved the way for Esther to become the next queen.

I love this story for a number of reasons, one of which is the fact that Esther was an orphan. *And he brought up Hadassah, that is, Esther, his uncle's daughter: for she had neither father nor mother... whom Mordecai, when her father and mother were dead, took for his own daughter* (Esth. 2:7). If this verse had been written in 21st century language, it may have read something like this: "Mordecai adopted his cousin, Esther, after her parents passed away, leaving her an orphan." Our family has become familiar with some of the emotions one might experience in the foster care system, and we have been blessed to know the amazing love associated with adoption. Mordecai must have experienced this love when he chose to adopt Esther and rear her as his own child. Therefore, I hope you will allow me the liberty to refer to Mordecai as Esther's daddy. As we study this story more closely, you will see the precious bond they shared, as evidenced by their actions toward one another.

Before we dive further into the book of Esther, I want to point out how near adoption is to the heart of God. He uses it to describe the relationship we have with Him once we have accepted Jesus Christ as our Saviour. *"But when the fulness of the time was come, God sent forth his Son, made of a woman, made under the law, To redeem them that were under the law, that we might receive the adoption of sons. And because ye are sons, God hath sent forth the Spirit of his Son into your hearts, crying, Abba, Father. Wherefore thou art no more a servant, but a son; and if a son, then an heir of God through Christ"* (Gal. 4:4-7). Then in James 1:27 we read: *"Pure religion and undefiled before God and the Father is this, To visit the fatherless and widows in their affliction, and to keep himself unspotted from the world."*

1. According to Psalm 10:14, what did God say He would do for the fatherless?

2. According to Psalm 68:4-5, God declared Himself to be what to the fatherless?

3. According to Psalm 82:3, what were judges commanded to do with reference to the fatherless?

I am a daddy's girl, and although my father provided me with very little spiritual leadership, he did provide me with a safe environment in which to grow, learn, and make decisions that would guide my future. Some of the decisions I made for myself were more conservative than the rules he had put in place for me, but he supported me in spite of his personal opinions. I have often said it was his love and acceptance of me that kept me from a life of sinful choices. I remember how happy he was when I chose to attend a Bible college where the students had a desire to serve those less fortunate, and how ecstatic he was when I married a preacher. As the story of the relationship between Mordecai and Esther progresses, we see the culmination of the years of Mordecai's investment in this relationship. I cannot help but smile as I think of the joy Mordecai must have felt when his Esther was chosen to be the next queen. *"And he brought up Hadassah, that is, Esther, his uncle's daughter: for she had neither father nor mother, and the maid was fair* (means "beautiful, comely: implies internal as well as external beauty; the form, shape, or appearance; fair of form") *and beautiful* (means "good"); *whom Mordecai, when her father and mother were dead, took for his own daughter"* (Esth. 2:7).

As I mentioned earlier, I love the story of Esther for a number of reasons, one of which is the insight we are given into God's purpose for creating Esther with such beauty. Had He not given Esther these features, she may not have been chosen as the next queen, and had she not been chosen to be queen, it could have changed the history of the Jewish nation. Beauty, like any other attribute, talent, or ability God has bestowed upon us, can be used to bring honor and glory to God, or to bring attention to ourselves. Esther did not allow her beauty to hinder her from humbling herself before God, nor to keep her from wisely heeding Mordecai's advice.

4. According to Esther 2:8-10, what did Mordecai suggest Esther keep to herself?

5. According to Esther 2:11, what did Mordecai do while he waited on the king's decision?

6. According to Esther 2:20, what did Esther continue to do after becoming queen?

Soon after Esther was chosen to be queen, Mordecai learned of a plot to murder the king. Because Mordecai had continued to build his relationship with Esther, he was able to pass on that information to Esther which saved the king's life. In the third chapter of Esther, we are introduced to a man named Haman, whom the king had promoted to the highest position of leadership in the kingdom, second only to himself. It was the custom in the land to bow in respect when in the presence of the king. Because of Haman's position, the people extended this same respect to him; however, Mordecai refused to bow. When questioned about his reason for not bowing, Mordecai testified that he was a Jew; his loyalty belonged to God alone and not to man. Of course, this angered Haman, and, in his anger, he conceived a plot to destroy not only Mordecai, but all of the Jews living in the Persian kingdom. The hearts of the Jewish people were smitten with grief as they learned of this plan, and Mordecai, clothed in sackcloth and ashes, led them in mourning. When news of Mordecai's mourning reached Esther, she sought to learn the reason.

Read Esther 4:3-17, and answer the questions below:

1. What was Mordecai's request of Esther?

2. What was Esther's concern?

3. What was Esther's final decision regarding this matter?

Our story continues as Esther prepares two different banquets before finally making her plea for the safety of her people. On the night before the second banquet, the king was unable to sleep. There is nothing like a good bedtime story, so he asked that the history books for his kingdom be read to him, which mentioned the time when Mordecai saved his life. When the king learned nothing had been done to honor Mordecai for his service, he asked Haman, *"What shall be done unto the man whom the king delighteth to honor"* (Esth. 6:6)? Thinking this honor would be directed to himself, Haman gave several suggestions only to be humiliated when learning the subject of this honor was his enemy, Mordecai. Later, when Queen Esther revealed Haman's wicked plan, he was further humiliated when the king sentenced him to death on the very gallows Haman had prepared for Mordecai.

4. Read Esther Chapter 8, and then give a summary of how this story concludes.

This unbelievable turn of events and amazing conclusion to a possible tragedy happened, in part, because a daddy decided to build a relationship with his little girl that lasted well into her adult years. May I remind you, Mordecai was not Esther's birth father. He chose to rear her as his very own; he chose to invest his time in her upbringing; he made the sacrifices necessary to lay the foundation upon which their relationship was built. Perhaps you are single, or a lady who was never given the opportunity to bear children. Perhaps you are a lady whose children are grown, and you have the impression that your child-rearing days are behind you. As long as we are here on this earth, God has a purpose for our lives. Perhaps He wants to use you to make a difference in the life of some young lady.

In the next few days, we will look specifically at some practical warnings regarding the potential pitfalls of physical beauty. My challenge is that we would choose to make the investments and sacrifices necessary in order to create a desire for those within our circle of influence to listen and heed these warnings.

In Proverbs 11:22 we read the following warning: *"As a jewel of gold in a swine's snout, so is a fair woman which is without discretion."* This verse is not speaking of an animated, adorable, pink pig with a sparkly, gold jewel in its nose. The picture drawn for us here is a fair (means "beautiful, comely: implying internal as well as external beauty") lady who is without discretion or good judgement being likened to a real-life, rolling-in-the-mud pig, that has a piece of gold jewelry in its snout. The idea of placing a gold ring in the nose of a pig sounds pretty funny; however, to see a beautiful lady who lacks discretion or good judgment is very disheartening. May this verse serve as a warning for us to *"Get wisdom, get understanding: forget it not; neither decline from the words of my mouth. Forsake her not, and she shall preserve thee: love her, and she shall keep thee. Wisdom is the principal thing; therefore get wisdom: and with all thy getting get understanding. Exalt her, and she shall promote thee: she shall bring thee to honour, when thou dost embrace her. She shall give to thine head an ornament of grace: a crown of glory shall she deliver to thee"* (Prov. 4:5-9). Wisdom is defined as "the ability to properly discriminate between good and evil, the receiving of instruction, and the exercising of correct judgment."

As I studied this week's topic, I couldn't help but think of the popular behavior females use called "flirting." Perhaps you have heard stories of those who have engaged in this practice to get out of a speeding ticket, or to gain an advantage in some other area of life. Flirting is a very unwise use of one's beauty that seeks to draw attention to oneself for the benefit of oneself. Friendliness, on the other hand, seeks to be kind and helpful to another and is a wise use of our resources. I would caution you to beware of the practice of flirting because it could bring upon you unwanted attention and consequences.

In Matthew 23:27 we are introduced to yet another warning: *"Woe unto you, scribes and Pharisees, hypocrites! for ye are like unto whited sepulchres, which indeed appear beautiful outward, but are within full of dead men's bones, and of all uncleanness."* The word "beautiful" in this verse "describes that which is seasonable, produced at the right time, as of the prime of life, or the time when anything is at its loveliest and best. It is used of the outward appearance of whited sepulchers in contrast to the corruption within." This passage goes on to say: *"Even so ye also outwardly appear righteous unto men, but within ye are full of hypocrisy and iniquity"* (Matt. 23:28). As we learned earlier in this study book, our behavior (thoughts, words, and actions) is a result of what we believe and what we desire. To illustrate this, do this simple exercise: Compare the time you spend preparing your outward appearance (fixing your hair, applying your make-up, etc.) to the time spent preparing your heart for the day in the Word of God. It is necessary to care for our outward appearance, but we would be wise to heed today's warning and focus on making the condition of our heart the greater priority.

We live in an amazing time in history when the Word of God is available to us in multiple formats. Perhaps as we prepare our outward appearance, we could also use the time to listen to Scripture, sermons, or to work on Bible memory. I personally practice all three of these, and it makes getting ready so much more enjoyable, especially since my appearance has been altered. Another idea would be to use our commute time to prepare our hearts. I recently heard about a gentleman who had a lengthy commute to and from work. It took him a couple of years, but he was able to memorize the entire book of Romans simply by listening to it as he drove. If we truly desire to be women of discretion, God will show us creative ways in which to incorporate more of the Word of God into our busy lives.

In the verses below, we have a wonderful example in the life of Abigail who, like Esther, was both beautiful and wise. Both of these ladies were married to men who held prominent positions, but were known for their tendency toward ruthless behavior. In 1 Samuel 25:3 we read: *"Now the name of the man was Nabal; and the name of his wife Abigail: and she was a woman of good understanding, and of a beautiful countenance: but the man was churlish and evil in his doings; and he was of the house of Caleb."* The word "beautiful" in this verse means "to be fair, comely in person, by nature or art; beautiful in action, in wisdom, in season, and in suitableness: it implies beauty internal as well as external." The words "good understanding" mean "to act prudently, intelligence, understanding, wisdom, success."

Read 1 Samuel 25:1-42, and answer the questions below:

1. What kind of man was Abigail's husband, Nabal?

2. How did Nabal respond to David's request for hospitality?

3. What kept David from slaughtering Nabal's household?

4. After years of living in a very difficult situation, how did God honor Abigail's behavior?

It was not Abigail's beauty that saved her husband's life and those of his household, neither did she flirt with David for a good outcome. We find that she humbly used good judgement to defuse what could have been a very bad situation. Oh, that we would see the need for wisdom in our own lives and desire it above riches! *"Happy is the man that findeth wisdom, and the man that getteth understanding. For the merchandise of it is better than the merchandise of silver, and the gain thereof than fine gold. She is more precious than rubies: and all the things thou canst desire are not to be compared unto her"* (Prov. 3:13-15).

Today, we will look at yet another warning regarding a potential pitfall of physical beauty. The stories we will read are more delicate in nature; therefore, I have chosen to be brief in my explanations. Because of this, you may choose to study them in more detail at a later date.

We live in a sinful world where some would take advantage of the physical beauty given by God for His purposes. This is nothing new as evidenced by the Word of God in the story of David and Bathsheba. Many would be familiar enough with this story to remember that David's choice to stay home rather than go to battle with his men resulted in an adulterous relationship that produced a child and ended with the murder of his loyal servant, Uriah. In 2 Samuel 11:1-2 we read the following: *"And it came to pass, after the year was expired, at the time when kings go forth to battle, that David sent Joab, and his servants with him, and all Israel; and they destroyed the children of Ammon, and besieged Rabbah. But David tarried still at Jerusalem. And it came to pass in an eveningtide, that David arose from off his bed, and walked upon the roof of the king's house: and from the roof he saw a woman washing herself; and the woman was very beautiful to look upon."* The word "beautiful," as it is used here to describe Bathsheba, simply means "good."

God, in His wisdom, allows us to see the sins of some of our Bible heroes, and David is no exception. While his behavior may have been acceptable for his position as king, it is obvious he knew his actions were contrary to the laws of God by the way in which he sought to hide his sin rather than confess and forsake it. There are many differing opinions regarding Bathsheba's participation in this sin, and after studying several opposing views, I felt it would be most beneficial to simply stay with what the Bible says. *"And when the mourning was past, David sent and fetched her to his house, and she became his wife, and bare him a son. But the thing that David had done displeased the LORD"* (2 Sam. 11:27). I found it interesting that God held David accountable for this sin. I also found it interesting that Bathsheba is listed as the wife of Uriah in Matthew's account of the genealogy of Jesus. *"And Jesse begat David the king; and David the king begat Solomon of her that had been the wife of Urias"* (Matt. 1:6). May this story serve as a warning to beware of men who choose their own fleshly desires over fulfilling their responsibilities. May it also serve as a warning to ladies to be aware of our surroundings and guard our modesty at all times.

Two chapters later we read another story involving David's family. Amnon, David's son, was advised by his friend, Jonadab, how to carry out the rape of his half-sister, Tamar. *"And it came to pass after this, that Absalom the son of David had a fair* (refers to both her inward and outer beauty) *sister, whose name was Tamar; and Amnon the son of David loved* (refers to his desire or lust) *her. And Amnon was so vexed, that he fell sick for his sister Tamar; for she was a virgin; and Amnon thought it hard for him to do any thing to her. But Amnon had a friend, whose name was Jonadab, the son of Shimeah David's brother: and Jonadab was a very subtil man"* (2 Sam. 13:1-3). This story records for us Tamar's protest against this sin and her attempt to encourage Amnon to go to his authority regarding the matter. It has been used by many leaders to warn young people about their choice of friends, but may it also serve as another warning to be aware of our surroundings. Amnon asked for the room to be cleared so he could be left alone with Tamar. This is a classic example of a situation we would want to avoid.

Many years ago, as I was locking some doors after a church service, I was approached by a man outside our building. It never occurred to me that I might be in a compromised situation. One of our male church members noticed the situation and stood nearby. When the conversation with the first gentleman concluded, I walked over to the second gentleman and asked if he needed help. I was so surprised when he told me he was actually there to assist me if needed. He then very kindly took it upon himself to accompany me safely back to my husband inside the building. We must be mindful of the fact that there are those who would try to take advantage of another's physical beauty regardless of the steps taken to protect oneself and refuse such advances. We would be wise to allow these stories to serve as warnings as we interact with the opposite gender.

Read the following practical suggestions and consider how you can incorporate them into your life.

1. First of all, I would like to encourage you to research a company by the name of R.A.D. Systems (www.rad-systems.com). This organization trains instructors across the nation to help ladies of all ages learn to be more aware of their surroundings and teaches the skills necessary to help them get out of a bad situation. When you go to the website, click on the "Program Locator" tab at the top, and then scroll down to find your state. This page contains a list of R.A.D. programs and web sites that provide R.A.D. Student Classes in your state. Please note this may only be a partial list. You would need to contact the Program Director for a complete list. Also, please keep in mind these instructors have full-time jobs besides their instructor duties; there may be a delay in their response to your inquiry for class dates and times. Many years ago, several ladies from our church participated in one of these classes. It was so tastefully done we repeated the class with our daughters. The following are some basic tools I learned and still practice to this day:

- Do not park beside a high-profile vehicle.

- Have your keys in your hand when you walk out of a place of business.

- Keep your head up and remain alert at all times when walking through a parking lot. If you notice anything suspicious upon approaching your vehicle, go back into the place of business and ask a security guard to accompany you.

- Ask a security guard to accompany you if it is dark outside and you feel at all uncomfortable. They are paid to do this, and I have found them very grateful for the opportunity to help.

- Rather than carrying your bags and packages, always use your shopping cart; it may serve as a barrier between you and a would-be attacker.

- Lock all the doors once you are safely in your vehicle.

- Do not use cutesy phrases on your license plates; they are like a target on your back.

- If you think someone is following you as you drive away, make three right turns. If you still feel you are being followed, do not drive home; drive to a well-lit, public place, and get help.

- Be sure all of the entrances to your home are free from any obstructions that would give an attacker a place to hide.

2. It is vitally important that we take time to educate our children. The following books can be purchased on-line. Even if you choose not to read them to your child, they are full of ideas and examples for role-playing with a child. When we take time to teach our children by role-playing, it gives them the confidence they need to say "NO"!

- *Do You Have a Secret? (Let's Talk About It!)* by Jennifer Moore-Mallinos

- *I Said No! A Kid-to-kid Guide to Keeping Private Parts Private* by Kimberly King

3. Schedule a day in the next couple of weeks to give yourself a modesty check-up. What was modest 20 pounds ago, may not be modest now. What you purchased before being made aware of this warning may not be what you want to wear now. Carve out a couple of hours for a "modesty check" - time to try on every garment in your wardrobe. If you are unsure of something, engage the help of another lady whom you feel exemplifies modesty. God-fearing husbands, dads, and brothers are good at giving this kind of advice, too. If you need help in discerning what is and what is not modest, I recommend the book *What Is Modesty? Discovering the Truth* by Michelle Brock (available on-line). It is a great little book that will take you on a journey from modesty of heart to modesty of body with several principles that can be applied to our daily choices of clothing.

Stop now and pray about each of these suggestions. Is there something you can begin to do today to keep yourself and those within your circle of influence from being a victim of those who prey upon the physical beauty given by God for His honor and glory?

As we consider today's warning, our main characters, Abram and Sarai, will undergo a name change during the time frame. Therefore, for the sake of clarity, I have chosen to use their new names, Abraham and Sarah. In Genesis 12:1-3, the Lord made Abraham a very significant promise when He said, *"...Get thee out of thy country, and from thy kindred, and from thy father's house, unto a land that I will shew thee: And I will make of thee a great nation, and I will bless thee, and make thy name great; and thou shalt be a blessing: And I will bless them that bless thee, and curse him that curseth thee: and in thee shall all families of the earth be blessed."* Following the Lord's command, Abraham journeyed to the land of Canaan, and after a time *"there was a famine in the land: and Abram went down into Egypt to sojourn there; for the famine was grievous in the land"* (Gen. 12:10). Abraham had enough faith to leave his homeland, but in verse 11 we find him taking matters into his own hands, rather than trusting the promise of protection that had been given to him by God. *"And it came to pass, when he was come near to enter into Egypt, that he said unto Sarai his wife, Behold now, I know that thou art a fair woman to look upon: Therefore it shall come to pass, when the Egyptians shall see thee, that they shall say, This is his wife: and they will kill me, but they will save thee alive. Say, I pray thee, thou art my sister: that it may be well with me for thy sake; and my soul shall live because of thee. And it came to pass, that, when Abram was come into Egypt, the Egyptians beheld the woman that she was very fair. The princes also of Pharaoh saw her, and commended her before Pharaoh: and the woman was taken into Pharaoh's house. And he entreated Abram well for her sake: and he had sheep, and oxen, and he asses, and menservants, and maidservants, and she asses, and camels. And the LORD plagued Pharaoh and his house with great plagues because of Sarai Abram's wife. And Pharaoh called Abram, and said, What is this that thou hast done unto me? why didst thou not tell me that she was thy wife? Why saidst thou, She is my sister? so I might have taken her to me to wife: now therefore behold thy wife, take her, and go thy way. And Pharaoh commanded his men concerning him: and they sent him away, and his wife, and all that he had"* (Gen. 12:11-20).

The Bible uses the word "fair" to describe Sarah, meaning she was "beautiful, comely, and implying internal as well as external beauty." It is very sad to realize Abraham concocted this plan out of a desire to protect himself rather than protect his wife. The rebuke given by Pharaoh should have been enough to bring Abraham and his wife to repentance for their lack of trust in the Lord and their willingness to solve this problem in a sinful way, but unfortunately, we find this scenario repeated with King Abimelech in Chapter 20. Not only was this scenario repeated, but according to verse 13, this was a premeditated sin that Abraham intended to practice on a regular basis. *"And it came to pass, when God caused me to wander from my father's house, that I said unto her, This is thy kindness which thou shalt shew unto me; at every place whither we shall come, say of me, He is my brother"* (Gen. 20:13).

Rather than choosing to protect his wife, Abraham chose to protect himself. This action is contrary to the biblical principal found in Philippians 2:3: *"Let nothing be done through strife or vainglory; but in lowliness of mind let each esteem other better than themselves."* As I was thinking about Sarah and her beauty, I could not help but wonder if this tendency to solve a problem in their own way was perhaps the foundation Sarah used when she offered Hagar to Abraham to bear the promised son. Jehovah God had given them several promises, and they willingly chose their own sinful way rather than taking Him at His Word.

In Chapter 26 of Genesis, we find this same sinful choice repeated in the life of Abraham's son, Isaac. Rebekah, Isaac's wife, is also referred to as being fair; however, the meaning of the word "fair" in this chapter simply refers to her goodness. I wonder if Isaac and Rebekah's story would have been different had Isaac grown up hearing of God's faithfulness and protection had his parents chosen to fully trust Him. Neither Sarah nor Rebekah chose to make a godly appeal to their husbands when asked to lie about their relationships, but instead chose to participate with them in the sin. As a result, both ladies were placed into compromising situations because of men who were first and foremost concerned for their own safety. In each situation, God graciously protected these women and used heathen men to rebuke their husbands. May these stories serve as a warning against selfishness, both in our own lives, and in the life of one with whom we may find an attraction.

Many years ago, I was privileged to meet an elderly couple who had been married for many years. When I asked them the secret to their successful marriage, they quickly replied with Romans 12:10: "*Be kindly affectioned one to another with brotherly love; in honour preferring one another.*" They went on to explain that many of the couples whom they had met seemed to love each other; however, they noticed they did not appear to prefer one another. There is a temptation to seek a relationship based solely upon physical attributes. In Week 3, I encouraged you to desire Christ-like attributes in your life. I trust the stories from the last two days will serve as a warning to look beyond physical attributes and seek Christ-like attributes in the life of any man in whom you have an interest. A woman of discretion would do just that!

1. According to 1 Corinthians 10:11-13, why are these stories so important for us to study?

2. According to Judges 2:7-10, what is the result when we fail to provide godly examples for the generations that follow us?

3. After reading today's lesson, is there someone from whom you need to seek forgiveness for acts of selfishness? Would you be willing to seek to make it right before the next week ends?

Today's warning is one with which many of us would be familiar. *"Favour is deceitful, and beauty is vain: but a woman that feareth the LORD, she shall be praised"* (Prov. 31:30). First, we will consider some definitions of the key words in this verse:

- Favor: "to be kindly and tenderly affected toward; to shew favor, mercy, pity."

- Deceitful: "a lie, a falsehood; a vain thing, that which deceives and disappoints hope."

- Beauty: "to be fair, beautiful, comely in person, by nature or art; beautiful in action, in wisdom, in season, and in suitableness: it implies beauty internal as well as external."

- Vain: "that which soon vanishes away, like vapor, or a bubble."

- Praised: "to shine, glorious, celebrated, praised."

- Feareth the Lord: "to have a sense of our own weakness, joined with trembling and reverence. It is an attitude of worship." In Noah Webster's 1828 Dictionary, the word "worship" is defined as "the act of paying divine honors to the Supreme Being; the reverence and homage paid to Him in religious exercises, consisting in adoration, confession, prayer, thanksgiving and the like." Years ago, my husband preached a series of sermons on this topic and used this simple explanation: "To fear God means to take Him seriously at his Word."

According to these definitions, this verse warns that kindness and favor can be given falsely, and physical beauty will vanish; however, a woman who takes God seriously at His Word shall shine; she shall be glorious; she shall be celebrated; she shall be praised. "The real worth of a woman is her devotion to God" (*Liberty Bible Commentary*).

"Above all, she fears the Lord. Beauty recommends none to God, nor is it any proof of wisdom and goodness, but it has deceived many a man who made his choice of a wife by it. But the fear of God reigning in the heart is the beauty of the soul; it lasts forever" (*Matthew Henry Commentary*). May these thoughts cause us to bow our hearts below our knees in humble submission to our Lord. We wrongly seek favor and beauty, when, instead, we should place the priority on seeking to fear the Lord.

Perhaps two of the most popular verses regarding the fear of the Lord are found in the book of Proverbs. *"The fear of the LORD is the beginning of knowledge: but fools despise wisdom and instruction"* (Prov. 1:7). *"The fear of the LORD is the beginning of wisdom: and the knowledge of the holy is understanding"* (Prov. 9:10). My husband made the following observations in his sermon series on the fear of the Lord: "The fear of God is the foundation upon which knowledge is built. Today, much knowledge is shared without the fear of God. This means any knowledge we gain should first be filtered through the Word of God in order to have the right perspective on that knowledge. For example, in Columbus' day, men said the earth was flat, yet the Bible speaks of the earth being circular, *'It is he that sitteth upon the circle of the earth...'* (Is. 40:22). Knowledge and wisdom are both different one from the other. Knowledge is the gathering of facts, but wisdom comes from viewing knowledge from God's perspective. Wisdom does not come just because a person gathers a great deal of knowledge. As Christians, we must take God seriously at what He says for this is not only the beginning of knowledge, but also wisdom, the proper way to use that knowledge." Next week we will spend a day looking more closely at wisdom, but today let us consider its predecessor, the fear of the Lord.

According to the following passages, what can we learn about the fear of the Lord?

1. Proverbs 8:13

2. Proverbs 15:31-33

3. Proverbs 19:23

4. Psalm 31:19-20

5. Job 28:12-28

Week Six

Beauty Truly Is in the Eye of the Beholder

Something to Think About

I am a "Plan A," "Plan B" type of person, meaning I can usually roll with the punches and quickly switch to "Plan B" if needed. I have even been known to have a "Plan C" tucked away in the event both of my first two plans fail. We have already established the fact that "If you fail to plan, you are planning to fail" (Benjamin Franklin). Having a plan and a back-up plan is actually a wise course of action; however, the way in which we react to switching from "Plan A" to "Plan B" reveals whether or not we are content in our situation. The very definition of the word "content," as stated in Noah Webster's 1828 Dictionary, means "having a mind at peace." Another definition from the same source is "to make quiet, so as to stop complaint or opposition." What a great thought! We are so prone to complain when things do not go as we had planned. Lastly, I thought this next definition was so applicable to today's lesson: "satisfaction which holds the mind in peace, restraining complaint…often implying a moderate degree of happiness." Before I share with you how God made this concept clear to me, we need to understand contentment as it is defined in the Word of God.

The following two verses use the same Greek word for "content" which means, "to be sufficient, to be possessed of sufficient strength, to be strong, to be enough for a thing." *"Let your conversation be without covetousness; and be content with such things as ye have: for he hath said, I will never leave thee, nor forsake thee"* (Heb. 13:5). *"And having food and raiment let us be therewith content"* (1 Tim. 6:8). As I thought about this definition, I could not help but realize the battle for contentment is in the mind. When I focus on the fact that God will never leave me, nor forsake me, and that He has provided me with more than enough food and clothing, it strengthens me to be content. However, if I focus on my hearing difficulty, the tightness in my face that occasionally causes my words to tumble out in a distorted fashion, my crooked smile, or droopy eye, I can be overcome with sadness from discontentment.

1 Timothy 6:6 tells us, *"But godliness with contentment is great gain."* The context of this verse is quite an eye opener in our "live to get more, have more, be more" world. The definition of contentment here simply means a "satisfaction with what one has." As I live with gratitude for all God has provided for me, it produces within me a heart of contentment. I can hear; I can speak; I can smile; and I can see. While I did wake up from surgery with some challenges, I do not have to deal with many of the complications that were a possibility. Once again, I must focus my mind on what God has provided for me.

I would like to share one last verse on the subject of contentment from the book of Philippians: *"Not that I speak in respect of want: for I have learned, in whatsoever state I am, therewith to be content"* (4:11). I was surprised to learn that the Greek word in this verse had a completely different meaning: "Sufficient in oneself, self-sufficient, adequate, needing no assistance." Paul had to learn contentment, just as I am learning. He learned through the experiences of *"...labours more abundant, in stripes above measure, in prisons more frequent, in deaths oft. Of the Jews five times received I forty stripes save one. Thrice was I beaten with rods, once was I stoned, thrice I suffered shipwreck, a night and a day I have been in the deep; In journeyings often, in perils of waters, in perils of robbers, in perils by mine own countrymen, in perils by the heathen, in perils in the city, in perils in the wilderness, in perils in the sea, in perils among false brethren; In weariness and painfulness, in watchings often, in hunger and thirst, in fastings often, in cold and nakedness"* (2 Cor. 11:23-27). Paul was totally dependent upon God; his satisfaction and sufficiency were in Christ alone. When I think of contentment in this context, I realize I still have very far to go in understanding and practicing this Christian grace.

How does one know if they are experiencing contentment as they switch from "Plan A" to "Plan B" or simply waiting for direction on the next step to take? Contentment comes when we believe God and take Him at His Word. He promises that we can know *that all things work together for good to them that love God, to them who are the called according to his purpose,"* and we know that purpose is *"to be conformed to the image of his Son"* (Rom. 8:28-29). When our plans are turned upside down, do we see God; do we trust God; do we rest in God's plan? This is why Week 2 may be the most important week in all of this study. A. W. Tozer was right when he said, "Our view of God determines our walk in life."

The Lord once again used a mountain climbing experience to make this truth real to me. In August of 2017, six months after my 60th birthday, I planned to hike a new mountain in honor of my new decade. Accompanying me on the hike was a young lady who had just graduated from high school and a young man with whom I had climbed several fourteeners. We would be hiking in the same area where I had climbed my very first fourteener with our two youngest sons, so I was feeling a wee bit sentimental. Huron Peak promised spectacular views, but there was a 40% chance of thunderstorms expected by noon. Because of my slow hiking pace, I normally would not have attempted a climb with this type of forecast. I simply do not like the pressure of trying to reach the summit and get off the mountain before a storm rolls in; however, this was the last opportunity the young man had before heading back to college. The young lady accompanying us had a time constraint as well which also caused me to feel concern over being able to summit. I immediately went into "Plan A," "Plan B" mode, reasoning that I might not be able to summit the mountain, but it would be an opportunity to invest in the lives of these young people. I must be honest and say that my heart was not near as excited about being able to invest in the lives of the young people as it was in being able to summit a new mountain in my new decade.

Prior to the hike, I had been discussing contentment with a friend, so the topic was fresh on my mind. During the hike, God began to do a transforming work in my heart. It has been my practice on other fourteener climbs to push hard to reach the summit; however, great disappointment came if circumstances kept me from doing so. As much as I wanted to reach the summit of this new peak, I felt overwhelmed with a desire to submit to whatever God would allow. Rather than pushing myself to reach a goal, I set out to enjoy the journey. I began to experience peace as I delighted in looking back to see how far I had come, focusing on all of the beauty around me. When I reached the ridge at 13,450 feet and realized we had only 30 minutes before we needed to begin our descent, I knew I was out of time to attempt the additional elevation gain of 553 feet. I called the young people, who were waiting at the summit, and told them to come back down. As I waited for them, I noticed I did not feel overcome with disappointment at not being able to summit. This time I was overwhelmed with joy because I had chosen to focus on what God allowed rather than what I felt I was missing. I thanked Him for the memories He allowed us to make before these young people headed out into the world to serve Him. I thanked Him for showing me the joy that comes when I simply surrender to His plans and for, once again, doing *"exceeding abundantly above all that we ask or think, according to the power"* that was working in me as I surrendered to Him.

In previous weeks, I have chosen not to give an assignment on Day 1. However, this week, I have added some additional material to assist you in learning to be content, whether in regard to your physical appearance, or any other area of your life.

Christian Contentment

By Debi Pryde

- Christian contentment is learned as we discover only Christ can satisfy the soul. *"Whom have I in heaven but thee? And there is none upon earth that I desire beside thee. My flesh and my heart faileth: but God is the strength of my heart, and my portion for ever"* (Ps. 73:25-26).

- Christian contentment is learned as we discover Christ is trustworthy and good. *"How excellent is thy loving kindness, O God! Therefore the children of men put their trust under the shadow of thy wings"* (Ps. 36:7).

- Christian contentment is learned as we discover Christ supplies all our needs. *"Cast thy burden upon the Lord, and He shall sustain thee..."* (Ps. 55:22).

- Christian contentment is learned as we make Christ's interests our first priority. *"But seek ye first the kingdom of God, and his righteousness; and all these things shall be added unto you"* (Mt. 6:33).

- Christian contentment is learned as we cultivate thankfulness. *"And let the peace of God rule in your hearts, to the which also ye are called in one body; and be ye thankful"* (Col. 3:15).

- Christian contentment is learned as we see life in light of eternity. *"For our light affliction, which is but for a moment worketh for us a far more exceeding and eternal weight of glory; while we look not at the things which are seen, but at the things which are not seen, for the things which are seen are temporal; but the things which are not seen are eternal"* (2 Cor. 4:17-18).

- Christian contentment is learned as we accept God's wise work in our lives. *"I know, O LORD, that thy judgments are right, and that thou in faithfulness hast afflicted me"* (Ps. 119:75). *"But now, O LORD, thou art our father; we are the clay, and thou our potter; and we all are the work of thy hand"* (Is. 64:8)

- Christian contentment is learned as we stop comparing our life to the lives of others. *"…but they measuring themselves by themselves, and comparing themselves among themselves, are not wise"* (2 Cor. 10:12).

- Christian contentment is learned as we grow in our understanding of who our God is, and know the unfathomable depth of God's love. *"O the depth of the riches both of the wisdom and knowledge of God! How unsearchable are his judgments, and his ways past finding out"* (Rom. 11:33)!

- Christian contentment is learned as we keep our focus on pleasing God rather than pleasing self, and on trusting God rather than putting trust in self or others. *"Thou wilt keep him in perfect peace, whose mind is stayed on thee: because he trusteth in thee"* (Is. 26:3).

- In the mid 1600's Jeremiah Burroughs wrote a book entitled *The Rare Jewel of Christian Contentment* in which is described contentment as "that sweet, inward, quiet, gracious frame of spirit, which freely submits to and delights in God's wise and fatherly disposal in every condition."

Ladies, contentment is a choice. As you are tempted to look into your mirror, wishing for different facial features may you choose to remember all you have learned about our God and accept His will over your own will. As we enter the final week in this study, it is my desire that you will gain a better understanding of the things God considers to be beautiful; each of them is attainable by all of us. May we choose to focus on the things the Lord has given us instead of the things He has not allowed us to have.

I found it rather interesting that God chose to assign a female pronoun to the word "wisdom" and teaches us that "she" is more valuable than silver, gold, and rubies. *"Happy is the man that findeth wisdom, and the man that getteth understanding. For the merchandise of it is better than the merchandise of silver, and the gain thereof than fine gold. She is more precious than rubies: and all the things thou canst desire are not to be compared unto her. Length of days is in her right hand; and in her left hand riches and honour. Her ways are ways of pleasantness, and all her paths are peace. She is a tree of life to them that lay hold upon her: and happy is every one that retaineth her"* (Prov. 3:13-18). Not only are these things valuable, they are also very beautiful. Perhaps you own a ruby ring or a special piece of silver. For many years, I had a simple gold chain that I loved to wear because I loved its simple beauty. Can you see the wisdom of God in comparing things of earthly beauty and value to those that have greater Heavenly value?

We have briefly discussed the need for wisdom in previous lessons, but today we will take a closer look at this valuable and beautiful attribute. God's Word clearly teaches how important it is to seek wisdom and how eager He is to grant it when we ask. *"Get wisdom, get understanding: forget it not; neither decline from the words of my mouth. Forsake her not, and she shall preserve thee: love her, and she shall keep thee. Wisdom is the principal thing; therefore get wisdom: and with all thy getting get understanding. Exalt her, and she shall promote thee: she shall bring thee to honour, when thou dost embrace her. She shall give to thine head an ornament of grace: a crown of glory shall she deliver to thee"* (Prov. 4:5-9). *"If any of you lack wisdom, let him ask of God, that giveth to all men liberally, and upbraideth not; and it shall be given him"* (Jas. 1:5).

What exactly is wisdom? In the Old Testament, it is often defined this way: "to discern, to perceive, the receiving of instruction and the exercising of good judgement, to act prudently." In the New Testament, it is often referred to as being prudent, which simply means to have understanding. In Week 5, Day 7, we learned the fear of the Lord is the beginning of wisdom; therefore, we cannot have wisdom if we do not take God seriously at His Word. Wisdom is a by-product of knowing and obeying the Word of God. It is the ability to apply the truths of the Word of God to our lives in a practical way.

Read the verses below, and in your own words write the evidences that should be present in the life of one who is filled with wisdom.

1. Proverbs 8:13

2. Proverbs 9:9

3. Proverbs 14:16

4. Proverbs 17:10

5. Daniel 12:3

6. Matthew 7:24

7. James 3:13-18

In my brief study of wisdom, I learned something I felt was very applicable to the subject of our physical appearance. In Ecclesiastes 8:1, we read the following: *"Who is as the wise man? and who knoweth the interpretation of a thing? a man's wisdom maketh his face to shine, and the boldness of his face shall be changed."* I absolutely love the explanation of this verse as given in the *Liberty Bible Commentary*: "The insight that wisdom brings to a man allows him to know the true interpretation to be placed upon events and brings a joy that is indicated in the shining of the face (Ps. 19:8). The hardness of the face, when viewed in the light of Deuteronomy 28:50 and Daniel 8:23, suggests a sinful and rebellious heart. The face then mirrors the personality. The shining countenance is a reflection of a new joy that has been born in a soul that has entered into the narrow way of wisdom." Oh, that we would desire to be women of wisdom!

How many times have you noticed a lady who did not necessarily have beautiful facial features, and yet, still appeared to be beautiful? This kind of beauty is an inner beauty which the Bible refers to as our countenance. In each of the following verses, the word "countenance" is defined as "the face…as expressing the affections or emotions of the mind." *"Why art thou cast down, O my soul? and why art thou disquieted within me? hope thou in God: for I shall yet praise him, who is the health of my countenance, and my God"* (Ps. 42:11; 43:5). *"A merry heart maketh a cheerful countenance: but by sorrow of the heart the spirit is broken"* (Prov. 15:13). These verses show us how our emotions affect our countenance.

A basic understanding of body chemistry reveals how the various choices we make can affect our emotions. For instance, physical exercise produces endorphins which release "happy hormones" into our system, which in turn affects the way we feel. The foods we eat also have a direct affect on the way we feel, and many would agree there is nothing like a good night's sleep to cause one to feel refreshed. However, it is important to understand that our thoughts also have a great impact on our body chemistry. While it is true that a sick body can affect our spirit, we must not allow the condition of our bodies to be an excuse not to glorify God in our spirit; we are commanded to use both to bring glory to Him. *"What? know ye not that your body is the temple of the Holy Ghost which is in you, which ye have of God, and ye are not your own? For ye are bought with a price: therefore glorify God in your body, and in your spirit, which are God's"* (1 Cor. 6:19-20). A good example of this would be those who suffer from some sort of debilitating disease or other physical ailment, yet exhibit a shining countenance. These folks do not allow the condition of their body to negatively affect their spirit. Our thought processes determine our spirit, and our spirit will be revealed in our countenance.

When we fail to see God in our circumstances, it is easy to fall prey to the emotions of anger, anxiety (fear), and/or depression. Since these emotions are not always sinful, let us take a few minutes and examine each of these in light of God's Word, so that we may recognize when they are a result of failing of obey one of God's commands. Proverbs 13:10 makes it very clear that sinful anger is rooted in pride: *"Only by pride cometh contention…"* We can gain further insight from James 4:1: *"From whence come wars and fightings among you? Come they not hence, even of your lusts that war in your members?"* As I was researching the next steps in the process of publishing this manuscript, I was honestly surprised by some of the requirements given by Christian publishing houses. For instance, in order to "be published," it is necessary to promote oneself. I was asked, "Do you have an online presence, and if so, how many followers do you have?" Yet Jesus tells us several times in the Gospels, *"If any man will come after me, let him deny himself, and take up his cross daily, and follow me"* (Luke 9:23). We are also admonished to, *"…follow after the things which make for peace, and things wherewith one may edify another"* (Rom. 14:19). In the few occasions where we are told to follow a man it is only in accordance to his following Christ. I then learned that many publishers require the author to have an agent. This is someone who will represent and promote the author; however, Psalm 75:6-7 tells us that, *"…promotion cometh neither from the east, nor from the west, nor from the south. But God is the judge: he putteth down one, and setteth up another."*

This is just a simple example of how easily we can become consumed with ourselves and filled with pride, thus laying the foundation for this very pointed statement given during a Women Counseling Women conference: "Clamor and anger and fighting come from the selfish and sinful desires within our own hearts. It is because of our pride, selfishness, and unloving hearts that we react to inconveniences, disappointments, the failures of others, hardship, and injustice with outrage instead of mercy, patience, acceptance, grace, love, or forgiveness."

In 2 Timothy 1:7 we are specifically told that, *"…God hath not given us the spirit of fear; but of power, and of love, and of a sound mind."* The Word of God reminds us many times to *"fear not"* as seen in Isaiah 41:10: *"Fear thou not; for I am with thee: be not dismayed; for I am thy God: I will strengthen thee; yea, I will help thee; yea, I will uphold thee with the right hand of my righteousness."* When we are tempted to be fearful we must apply the Word of God to our lives. When I read, *"Fear thou not; for I am with thee…"* I must stop and ask myself, "Who is with me?" "What do I know about Him?" "How has He helped me in the past?" "Do I believe Him?" "Can I trust Him?" Fear comes as a result of failing to take God at His Word.

Prior to my surgery, I was given a list of possible complications to read before signing the surgical consent form. As I read them, I could feel my heart begin to fill with fear, so about half way through I stopped reading. I looked up at my nurse and asked, "Did we not just come to the conclusion that I have no other options?" When she replied in the affirmative, I asked permission to sign the form without reading any further. Within the next few days, I did finish reading the list, and then made the decision to allow the fear to motivate me to prepare for any one of those complications instead of allowing it to paralyze me. I had the most productive weeks of my life leading up to my surgery. When I left our home to travel to the hospital, I did so with joy in my heart knowing that I would be coming home to a comfortable place to recover. I also knew that if anything were to happen where I could no longer function as "home-maker," it would be easy for my husband to take over.

I also asked the Lord for a verse, or a passage, upon which to focus in those scary moments when I would be wheeled away from my family members and into a cold, sterile room where lots of busy nurses and doctors would be making final preparations. The Lord gave me Psalm 23. I had to chuckle since it is often the Psalm read at funerals, but the Lord knows how much I love to think of Him as my Shepherd. I love standing at the top of our Rocky Mountains, but I told my daughter I would be falling asleep while resting with my Shepherd in green pastures.

Depression is another emotion that will affect our countenance. Although the word "depression" is not in the Bible, the concept of depression is seen in the words "cast down," "troubled," "overwhelmed," and "despair." It is normal in life to experience sadness, but this is beyond the definition most of us refer to when we say we are feeling depressed. Please allow me to once again share a quote from a Women Counseling Women conference: "The Bible teaches that such a mental condition is often the reflection of a state of mind in which an individual focuses on real or imagined problems, difficulties, perils, or losses with a perspective of defeat and despair. When this occurs, it is more than sorrow - it is sorrow without hope." Once again we can find direction and comfort in the Word of God: *"Be of good courage, and he shall strengthen your heart, all ye that hope in the LORD"* (Ps. 31:24).

I find it so very precious how God cared for Elijah after his amazing victory over the prophets of Baal on Mount Carmel. He declared the LORD to be God and witnessed a miracle as *"...the fire of the LORD fell, and consumed the burnt sacrifice, and the wood, and the stones, and the dust, and licked up the water that was in the trench. And when all the people saw it, they fell on their faces: and they said, The LORD, he is the God; the LORD, he is the God"* (1 Kings 18:38-39). But then we read in the very next chapter, the great prophet Elijah became so depressed that he begged the Lord to take his life. Instead, the Lord Who *"...knoweth our frame; he remembereth that we are dust"* (Ps. 103:14), sent an angel to minister to Elijah. The angel fed him, gave him something to drink, allowed him to sleep some more, and then fed him again before sending him on his way.

Do you desire to have a beautiful countenance? Notice I did not say, "Do you desire to have beautiful facial features?" God planned your features long before you were conceived, and no matter what our facial features are, we can have a beautiful countenance. We will need to get enough exercise, make good choices about the things we eat, get a good night's sleep, and change our thinking when we recognize sinful emotions are controlling us.

Today's lesson was rather lengthy, but the truth is each of these emotions should be explored in further detail, particularly if you find yourself struggling with them. I would encourage you to visit www.debipryde.com. Not only will you be blessed by the many free handouts, but you will also find a list of several helpful Bible study tools. In relation to our study today, I would like to recommend the following books: *Why Am I So Angry*, *Why Am I So Depressed*, and *Secrets of a Happy Heart*.

As we conclude today's lesson, let us consider what the Word of God has to say about these emotions that affect our countenance.

1. According to 2 Corinthians 10:5, what are we to do with our thoughts?

2. According to Hebrews 4:12, what is the final judge of my thoughts?

3. According to Philippians 4:6-8, rather than feeling "careful," or anxious, upon what should we focus our thinking?

4. According to Proverbs 25:28, how do you believe God wants us to deal with our anger?

5. According to Psalms 16:8-9, 146:5, and Romans 15:13 what emotion can we expect to experience as we place our hope in the Lord?

I was delighted to learn of yet another area God considers to be beautiful. In Psalm 16:5-7 we read: *"The LORD is the portion of mine inheritance and of my cup: thou maintainest my lot. The lines are fallen unto me in pleasant places; yea, I have a goodly heritage. I will bless the LORD, who hath given me counsel: my reins also instruct me in the night seasons."* The word "goodly" means "fair, shining, pleasant, acceptable, beauty." As I write, I am recovering from an accident in which a jackknifed truck totaled my husband's car which was purchased with the inheritance left to him by his father. However, his father left him far more than the proceeds from his tiny home; he left him the legacy of a humble, hard-working, simple man. We have no control over what is given to us as an inheritance, but we can control what we pass on to the next generation. You may be thinking, "I am a single lady and have no one to whom I can pass a heritage." Please allow me to emphatically say, "Oh, yes you do!" I have a daughter-in-law who has been greatly influenced by a single aunt. I have not met her personally; however, I have learned from her dedication to her nieces and nephews. At the close of today's lesson, I have listed for you some resources written by single ladies who have made a profound impact upon my life. None of them had any idea how their lives would continue to challenge women far beyond their graves, and neither do we. A goodly heritage is something beautiful we can pass to the next generation.

In the verse above, the Psalmist is actually rejoicing in the fact that the Lord is his inheritance. When a person places his/her faith in Christ, he/she becomes a child of God. What a precious thought to realize our Heavenly Father has given us a "goodly heritage." However, thoughts of our earthly heritage can remind us of a difficult past. I have given much praise to my father throughout this study and have alluded to a less than perfect relationship with my mother. I spent far too much time sitting in my closet as a child weeping over what I perceived to be a lack of love from my mother. I felt as though I was to blame for her mistreatment of me. After she passed away, my father acknowledged the mistreatment; however, he had no explanations for it, only sincere sorrow. There is no need to go into detail, and, to be honest, my situation would be minor in comparison to many. The truth is my mother was a good woman, who gave birth to four children within a five-year time frame and worked a full-time job outside the home, which allowed my father to run his own business. I had been so consumed with how she hurt me that it took me a long time to be able to see the good in the heritage she left. What opened my eyes and allowed me to see the good? Forgiveness. Forgiveness can free a person from a hurtful past, but forgiveness can be difficult to understand. As we consider the goodly heritage left to us by Jesus Christ, let us choose to follow His example of forgiveness.

The word "forgiveness" in the Bible has several meanings, but overall, it simply means to release your offender of the debt he/she owes you. In Matthew's account of the Lord's Prayer, we read the following: *"And forgive us our debts, as we forgive our debtors. And lead us not into temptation, but deliver us from evil: For thine is the kingdom, and the power, and the glory, for ever. Amen"* (Matt. 6:12-13). The words "debt" and "debtor" refer to the need one has to make amends for wrongdoing, or to pay for sin by way of punishment. When someone sins against us in some way, then recognizes his/her sin against us, and seeks our forgiveness, it is fairly easy to forgive. You may be asking, "But what should I do when my offender does not seek my forgiveness?" The biblical command is to forgive them anyway. *"And when ye stand praying, forgive, if ye have ought against any: that your Father also which is in heaven may forgive you your trespasses"* (Mark 11:25). *"For thou, Lord, art good, and ready to forgive; and plenteous in mercy unto all them that call upon thee"* (Ps. 86:5). God has forgiveness ready for us, and we are commanded to have forgiveness ready for our offenders. We are commanded to be ready to forgive those who do not confess their sin toward us, but rather make excuses, justify their actions, or simply refuse to admit any wrongdoing when confronted about the offense.

How can we be ready to forgive? Let us look further at God's example of forgiveness. In Isaiah 43:25 we read: *"I, even I, am he that blotteth out thy transgressions for mine own sake, and will not remember thy sins."* We see this truth repeated in Jeremiah 31:34: *"And they shall teach no more every man his neighbour, and every man his brother, saying, Know the LORD: for they shall all know me, from the least of them unto the greatest of them, saith the LORD: for I will forgive their iniquity, and I will remember their sin no more."* In both verses, we learn the key to being ready to forgive. God does not say He forgets our sins; He says that He chooses not to remember our sins. These are two different acts. The act of forgetting is a passive act - something that happens by chance. The act of choosing not to remember is something we do deliberately and on purpose. If we are to have forgiveness ready for those who have sinned against us, we must stop ourselves from dwelling on the offense when it comes to our minds.

When we choose to dwell on the sins committed against us, bitterness begins to grow in our hearts. We are warned in Hebrews 12:15, *"Looking diligently lest any man fail of the grace of God; lest any root of bitterness springing up trouble you, and thereby many be defiled."* Bitterness is the result of being hurt and refusing to deal with the hurt biblically. At the moment we are offended, we have a choice to make. We can choose to forgive our offender, or we can choose to dwell on the hurt over and over until we become bitter. The Bible actually teaches there are some offenses we are to forbear, or pass over. *"Put on therefore, as the elect of God, holy and beloved, bowels of mercies, kindness, humbleness of mind, meekness, longsuffering; Forbearing one another, and forgiving one another, if any man have a quarrel against any: even as Christ forgave you, so also do ye"* (Col. 3:12). Many of the offenses that come our way are not actually sins committed against us, and in these cases we must simply forbear. However, if we continue to replay the situation over and over in our minds, we should confront our offender and seek reconciliation, remembering it is our responsibility to forgive regardless of the response we receive. Forgiveness is an act of our wills, not our emotions. We forgive in obedience to God.

Read the verses below, and answer the following two questions:

1. According to Matthew 6:9-15, what is the consequence of refusing to forgive our offenders?

2. According to Matthew 18: 21-35, how often should we forgive our offenders?

If you are struggling with forgiveness, you may find it helpful to read the following true stories of those who have also struggled, but who have emerged victorious.

- *Dorie, The Girl Nobody Loved* by Doris Van Stone with Erwin W. Lutzer. When Doris Van Stone was just a child, she lived a life of physical and emotional abuse, being told on a daily basis that she was an ugly child. Her story is an amazing testimony of how even a child can develop a relationship with Jesus

Christ and a deep love for the Word of God that will sustain him/her through horrific trials. Doris was greatly impacted by, and then served with, missionary Darlene Deibler Rose.

- *Evidence Not Seen* by Darlene Deibler Rose. Mrs. Rose learned forgiveness in her 20's in a Japanese prison camp in the jungles of New Guinea during World War 2. I am sure that as she suffered tremendous abuse, she never imagined how her life would impact the lives of others, including a future co-laborer.

- *The Hiding Place*, and its sequel *Tramp for the Lord* by Corrie ten Boom. Miss Boom was in her 50's when she was arrested and placed into one of Hitler's death camps. You would think after surviving the death camp there would be no more trials for Miss Boom; however, God continued to give her opportunities to learn to forgive even into her 80's.

If you are a single lady, you may be inspired by the legacy left by other single ladies. The following ladies were just regular women who used their single status to bring honor and glory to God and have inspired women of all stations in life.

- Gladys Aylward, who was never considered "qualified" to serve on the mission field, yet was used of the Lord to make a profound impact upon the people of China.

- Amy Carmichael, who served as a missionary to India for 55 years without a furlough, wrote many inspiring books. She became bedridden due to an accident in her 60's, but stayed on her mission field and wrote an additional 16 books before she went on to Heaven.

- Hannah Hurnard, in her early years penned the Christian classic, *Hinds' Feet on High Places*. I believe God used her to inspire me to climb to the high places where He has often challenged me to new heights spiritually. Please allow me to share one of her quotes regarding being single:

"It is God's will that some of His children should learn this deep union with Himself through the perfect flowering of natural human love in marriage. For others it is equally His will that the same perfect union should be learned through the experience of learning to lay down completely this natural and instinctive desire for marriage and parenthood, and accept the circumstances of life which deny them this experience. This instinct for love, so firmly implanted in the human heart, is the supreme way by which we learn to desire and love God Himself above all else."

Today I would like to look at yet another aspect of beauty, one upon which the Lord places a great deal of emphasis. *"Give unto the LORD the glory due unto his name: bring an offering, and come before him: worship the LORD in the beauty of holiness"* (1 Chron. 16:29). *"And when he had consulted with the people, he appointed singers unto the LORD, and that should praise the beauty of holiness, as they went out before the army, and to say, Praise the LORD; for his mercy endureth for ever"* (2 Chron. 20:21). *"Give unto the LORD the glory due unto his name; worship the LORD in the beauty of holiness"* (Psalm 29:2). In the previous verses, the word "beauty" means "glory, honor, majesty, splendor, beauty and ornament." The *Liberty Bible Commentary* says, "Although this may mean to worship Him in the vestments of the priests, it more likely means that we are to worship Him in a holy ornament of meekness and a quiet spirit."

Since holiness and a meek and quiet spirit are beautiful qualities we can possess, we will look at them more closely today. The word "holiness" in the verses above simply means "to be pure, clean, sacred." In 2 Peter 3:10-12, we read the following: *"But the day of the Lord will come as a thief in the night; in the which the heavens shall pass away with a great noise, and the elements shall melt with fervent heat, the earth also and the works that are therein shall be burned up. Seeing then that all these things shall be dissolved, what manner of persons ought ye to be in all holy conversation and godliness, Looking for and hasting unto the coming of the day of God..."* The word "holy" in this passage means to be "separated from sin and therefore consecrated to God, sacred." As Christians, we believe the truth that Jesus is coming back for us, but so often we forget this in our day-to-day activities.

Many years ago, the Lord revealed to me my failure to live in light of His imminent return. At the time, we were living in a rented home and our children were very young. My husband had contacted our landlord and informed him that our bathtub faucet was in need of repair. He responded by telling us he would make the repair "sometime during the weekend." SOMETIME THIS WEEKEND? Did he not realize we had four young children? I stressed over how to keep every room in our home clean for his arrival. I began to vacuum after instructing the children to clean their rooms. After a few moments, one of the boys returned and asked me why he had to clean his room since the landlord was only coming to fix the bathroom faucet. I explained to him that the landlord owned the house we were living in which gave him the right to enter any room to see how we were caring for his property. As I returned to my vacuuming, the thought hit me: Jesus is coming! He could return at any minute! My Lord owns me, and He has the right, at any time, to examine every "room" in my heart.

The passages below will help us keep holy living in the forefront of our minds. Read each of them, and answer the questions that follow.

1. According to 1 John 3:2-3, what will the hope of Jesus' coming do for us?

2. According to Psalm 139:23-24, what prayer should regularly be on our lips and in our hearts to be ready for His coming?

In Matthew 11:28-29, Jesus invites us to *"Come unto me, all ye that labour and are heavy laden, and I will give you rest. Take my yoke upon you, and learn of me; for I am meek and lowly in heart: and ye shall find rest unto your souls."* The word "meek" simply means "gentle or mild." Gentleness and meekness are both noted as a fruit of the Spirit in Galatians 5:22-23. Then, in 1 Peter 3:1-4, we are admonished to possess a quiet spirit: *"Likewise, ye wives, be in subjection to your own husbands; that, if any obey not the word, they also may without the word be won by the conversation of the wives; While they behold your chaste conversation coupled with fear. Whose adorning let it not be that outward adorning of plaiting the hair, and of wearing of gold, or of putting on of apparel; But let it be the hidden man of the heart, in that which is not corruptible, even the ornament of a meek and quiet spirit, which is in the sight of God of great price."* The definition of a quiet spirit is "tranquility arising from within, causing no disturbance to others." It is important not to mistake a meek and quiet spirit for a personality trait. A woman can have an outgoing, or fun-loving personality and still possess a meek and quiet spirit. For example, I know several women who are nurses or first responders. These women are often called upon to make quick, life-saving decisions that require them to give orders to those assisting them, but at the same time maintain a calm, peaceful exposure and a gentle disposition to the patient.

According to the verses at the beginning of today's lesson, it is a beautiful thing when we worship our Heavenly Father with clean hearts and gentle, peaceful spirits. In light of this, I thought it would be good for us to examine the confession that comes from true godly repentance. Read Psalm 51, and answer the questions below:

3. How did David approach God in verses one and two?

4. What did David willingly admit in verses three and four?

5. Beginning with verse eight and continuing through the end of the chapter, David showed he was not only interested in having his sins forgiven but also in having his fellowship with God restored. Using your own words, make a list of David's petitions that reveal his desire to worship God in holiness with a meek and quiet spirit.

As we near the end of this study, I felt it would be good to remind us that we are here on this earth, created with both our physical attributes and our individual personalities, to bring glory to God. Our purpose is to live in the power of His Spirit, so that we might love Him with all our heart, soul, mind, and strength, and to love others as ourselves. He came with the purpose *"to seek and to save that which was lost"* (Luke 19:10), and desires for us to do the same. In Isaiah 52:7 we read: *"How beautiful upon the mountains are the feet of him that bringeth good tidings, that publisheth peace; that bringeth good tidings of good, that publisheth salvation; that saith unto Zion, Thy God reigneth!"* Then in Romans 10:15 we read: *"And how shall they preach, except they be sent? as it is written, How beautiful are the feet of them that preach the gospel of peace, and bring glad tidings of good things."* Here, the word "beautiful" means "that which is seasonable, produced at the right time, as of the prime of life, or the time when anything is at its loveliest and best."

Our son, Dave, currently works with an organization that seeks to take the audio version of the Word of God to people groups who have not yet heard the good news of the gospel of Jesus Christ. As I write this lesson, he and his boss are in West Africa to do just that. What a thrill it has been to watch the various videos he has shared of small groups of people huddled together listening to the Word of God in their native tongue. I thought it was interesting that the *Liberty Bible Commentary* interpreted the text in Romans 10:15 to mean "the feet of a gospel messenger are beautiful things to those who believe the message and place their faith in the Lord Jesus." How many times have we listened in awe as missionaries return from their fields of service to give us updates of their ministries? They tell how quickly the Word of God is snatched up by those who have never seen, or held a copy, or even a portion thereof, and our eyes fill with tears. What a precious gift we sometimes take for granted! The men and women, who have given their lives to take the gospel around the world, have beautiful feet, and ours can be beautiful, too.

While it may be a popular practice to get a pedicure in order to beautify our toenails for our summer sandals, it is becoming less and less popular to beautify our feet by sharing the gospel of Jesus Christ. I do not know how long we will be able to enjoy our freedom to worship in our country, but I do know it is still God's plan for us to share the gospel. We must be creative and use the various resources we have. You may have heard the phrase, "People don't care what you know until they know that you care." Perhaps we need to slow down our busy lives so we can see and meet the needs of those around us. We must take the time necessary to build relationships with our neighbors and those with whom we do business. If there was ever a time when Christians needed to care about the souls of lost men and women, that time is now! In this emotionally unattached, electronic world, it is imperative that people know we care, in order to be able to introduce them to a relationship with Jesus Christ.

1. According to Proverbs 11:30, and Daniel 12:3, what is a basic characteristic of those who seek to win lost souls?

2. According to 1 Corinthians 9:16-27, what is Paul willing to do in order to win lost souls?

3. According to Matthew 28:18-20, what was Jesus' final request of His followers?

Today's topic of God-given beauty is one that many choose to cover up: gray hair, aka, growing old. Coloring our hair can add a youthful look to our appearance; however, it was really an encouragement to me to read what God says about our graying hair. *"The glory of young men is their strength: and the beauty of old men is the gray head"* (Prov. 20:29). I think this can apply to women too! The meaning of the word "beauty" in this verse is "that which is seasonable, produced at the right time, as of the prime of life, or the time when anything is at its loveliest and best." I love this definition in light of the context of this verse. Have you ever heard the senior season of life referred to as the "prime of life," or the "loveliest and best"? Many humorous things have been said about getting older, and the greeting card industry has certainly contributed with its comical and sarcastic remarks. However, God sees beauty in this season of our lives.

As we age, life can become challenging. Not only is it challenging for us as senior citizens, but it can be challenging for our caregivers as well. I did not have the responsibility of caring for aging parents because they died so young, but I do have friends who have risen to meet that challenge. I admire them for their dedication and service to their elderly parents. We have all met "old" people whom we adore, but the opposite is also true. With that thought in mind, I would like to recap this week's lessons by suggesting a goal for which each of us can strive.

Imagine for a moment, you have reached that time in your life when you are considered a senior citizen. Your hair is graying, becoming coarser, or perhaps even thinning. As you look into the mirror and see the changes, not only to your hair, but also to your aging body, you smile with a contented heart. You have lived a life that has had many challenges, but you have allowed those challenges to cause you to seek a deeper relationship with the Lord. Through it all, you have learned that God is enough. He has done so much for you, and you are able to trust that He will continue to do just what you need as you continue your journey to meet Him. Through the challenges you have faced, you learned to rely upon God and seek Him for wisdom to properly interpret life's events and to make right choices. You have seen Him answer your prayers in big ways and in the smallest of ways. You have been able to observe His tender care in the things that are important to you; therefore, you feel no anxiety, or anger, over the things in your life that did not follow your plan. Even in your heartaches, there was an inner peace because of your confidence in your Heavenly Father. You have surrounded yourself with others who have chosen to count their blessings rather than their ailments, and together you find many things that bring joy and laughter. You are tempted to chuckle when others comment on your beauty because you know it faded many years ago. They may talk about the sparkle in your eyes, the softness of your skin, the kindness that pours from your lips, and the sweetness in your spirit, but you know it wasn't always that way. You remember the conviction, the times of repentance, and the sweet restoration that made you *"draw nigh to God"* (Jas. 4:8). They know there are certain things about which you will not jest because they would not be pleasing to the Lord. They also know if they share a personal struggle, you will most likely quote a Bible verse, or biblical principle, while offering a book suggestion. They have the confidence you will pray for them, whether or not you have any answers, because you know the One who does. They know you would want them to have a gospel tract ready in case there is an opportunity to witness to your doctor or hospice nurse. When the day finally arrives when your loved ones lay you to rest, they may briefly remember the challenges, but they will rejoice in the legacy you have left behind. Hopefully, just maybe, they will have been able to see a little bit of Jesus in you. This, my friend, is a beauty within reach of us all.

I have just one assignment for you today: think about your life. It does not matter what age you are, or how far you have come in your walk with God; we can all make adjustments to our lives in the areas we studied this week. What change, or changes, do you need to make so your loved ones will one day praise the Lord for the beautiful legacy you have left behind? Write your decision below.

Epilogue

Just a few days after my surgery, my friend, Becky Pope, sent me a rather lengthy Bible study from Galatians 6:17: *"From henceforth let no man trouble me: for I bear in my body the marks of the Lord Jesus."* She made the following statements in regard to her battle with cancer: "I was comforted at the thought that my scars were what the Lord chose for me - marks of His ownership of me... I was reading from my Bible study program about this verse, where Paul mentions his scarring from the scourgings. No doubt, the man was covered with scars, and some believe that he had a continual running of drainage from his eyes as a result of being struck blind at the time of his conversion. Paul saw his scars and wounds as the results of enduring what Christ had chosen for him, proof that he was Christ's and none others."

I was so appreciative of her comforting words to me that I added to them the following explanation given in the *Liberty Bible Commentary*: "There were devotees who stamped upon their bodies the names of the gods whom they worshiped; some slaves had the names or marks of their owners on their bodies, and sometimes soldiers were thus identified. Paul glorified in being a slave of Jesus Christ. The brand marks, his badge of lifelong, faithful service were the scars left by scourgings, stones at Lystra, and rods at Philippi. Paul had endured hardness as a good soldier of Jesus Christ." As stated earlier in this study, he did so by the grace of God, and that is the only way, we too, will *"endure hardness as a good soldier of Jesus Christ"* (2 Tim. 2:3).

Isaiah Chapter 53 contains a well-known Old Testament prophecy which describes the sufferings Jesus would face in order to atone for our sin. At the very beginning of this passage, God makes it clear to us that there is nothing about Jesus' physical appearance that we would desire. *"For he shall grow up before him as a tender plant, and as a root out of a dry ground: he hath no form nor comeliness; and when we shall see him, there is no beauty* (appearance) *that we should desire him"* (Is. 53:2). As I considered this thought, I remembered Paul's desire to know Christ, and to know Him in the fellowship of His sufferings. *"But what things were gain to me, those I counted loss for Christ. Yea doubtless, and I count all things but loss for the excellency of the knowledge of Christ Jesus my Lord: for whom I have suffered the loss of all things, and do count them but dung, that I may win Christ, And be found in him, not having mine own righteousness, which is of the law, but that which is through the faith of Christ, the righteousness which is of God by faith: That I may know him, and the power of his resurrection, and the fellowship of his sufferings, being made conformable unto his death"* (Phil. 3:7-10).

While there are many of us who have had our appearance altered due to one circumstance or another, there are those who have endured much emotional and/or physical trauma because of their witness for Christ. One year after my surgery, I attended a conference hosted by Voice of the Martyrs (VOM) and heard a story that gripped my heart. I knew at that moment God would have me use the story to conclude this Bible study. This story is true, but I do want to warn you, the content is graphic. It is used by permission from Petr Jasek, a Global Ambassador with Voice of the Martyrs from his book *Imprisoned with ISIS: Faith in the Face of Evil.* May it serve as one final challenge for us to have the proper perspective regarding our physical appearance.

In July 2009, Monica and her husband were riding on a motorcycle through the city of Maiduguri in Northern Nigeria. It was a Thursday, and they were on their way to their church to attend a Bible study. As they traveled, though, Islamic militants wearing camouflaged military uniforms and masks flooded the road and blocked their path. The men carried long, sharp machetes and machine guns. Monica and her husband knew these men were members of Boko

Haram, the jihadi terrorist group who had been rampaging northern Nigeria.

"What is your religion?" one of the militants demanded, stepping forward menacingly with his machete in his hand. "We are Christians," Monica and her husband boldly replied. "You can save your lives by becoming Muslims," the militant said. "Repeat the shahada," he insisted, referring to the Muslim profession of faith. But the two Christians refused. "We are Christians," they said, "and we remain Christians."

The Boko Haram militant raised his machete, and in three swift slices, severed Monica's husband's head from his body. Knowing her husband was dead, and that there was nothing she could do to help him, she ran. The men chased her, slicing at her back with a sharp machete. Soon, she felt a heavy hand on her shoulder. She had been caught. The angry militant spun her around and sliced her throat with his machete. Monica fell to the ground, blood gushing from her neck, and within seconds she lost consciousness. The men, assuming she was dead as well, tossed her body into a sewer where she lay for the next two and a half hours. As she was lying unconscious in the ditch, she saw heavenly beings dressed in white surrounding her.

Finally, members of the village police came through to identify the victims of Boko Haram's most recent attack and bury the bodies. They came to Monica's body and lifted her from the ditch, but to their surprise, she started to move. Using sign language, Monica asked for some water. One of the policemen gave her water to drink, but it dribbled out through the cut in her throat. The police brought Monica to the local hospital where she underwent a series of several surgeries. Doctors implanted a device in her throat through a tracheotomy so that she could breathe; when covering the hole in the device with her finger, she could even speak in a whisper.

I remembered clearly the first time I met Monica. VOM had sent me to meet her and to see how we might offer medical aid to her. I was so moved by the story of her husband's murder and the vicious attack against her and the boldness with which they had both declared their faith in Christ. My colleague from the Mayo Clinic in the US was reviewing her medical history as I prepared questions for my interview and documented her injuries with my camera. I felt a tremendous burden for her and struggled to find the right question with which to begin my interview.

Eventually, I dared to ask her a simple question: "Monica," I asked, "how are you doing in the Lord? How has your relationship with the Lord changed after this horrific experience?" I will never forget her answer. Before she could speak, Monica took a deep breath then closed the hole in her throat device with her index finger so that air could pass through her damaged vocal cords. Finally, in a raspy voice modulated by the device in her throat, she whispered: "I focus my eyes on eternity." She removed her finger, took another deep breath, and then continued. "I focus my eyes on Jesus."

Through breathy, pained whispers, Monica told me that before the attack, she had considered herself and her husband "good" Christians. But, she told me, she had been so concerned with buying a new dress and working hard to save money to buy a nice car or house. Now, after her husband's death and her own miraculous deliverance, she wanted to dedicate her whole life to serving Jesus. In fact, soon after her final surgery, Monica began the dangerous, brave work of helping VOM in assisting other widows who had lost their husbands in similar ways to Boko Haram militants. Twice, VOM has had to relocate her when her life was in danger.

God used Monica's words to once again remind me to focus on the mirror of God's Word rather than the reflection I see in the mirrors hanging in our home. As we close this study, may we ask ourselves, upon what is my focus? Do I focus on whether or not others see value in me? Is my focus on the things I possess, or on the reflection I see in the mirror? It is my desire that each one of us would walk away from this six-week study saying with Monica, "I focus my eyes on eternity. I focus my eyes on Jesus."

Answer Key

Week One

Week 1, Day 2

1. Jesus Christ, His blood
2. The curtain between the Holy Place and the Holy of Holies was torn into two pieces.
3. It symbolized the fact that we now have access to God through our High Priest, Jesus Christ.

Week 1, Day 3

1. It reveals the problem I need to correct.
2. No
3. We are redeemed by the precious blood of Jesus Christ.

Week 1, Day 4

1. Write out your personal testimony.

Week 1, Day 5

1. I can go to my Heavenly Father and seek His help with any need I have.
2. Jesus will never leave me, nor forsake me.
3. Jesus is my good Shepherd; He will watch over me and care for me.

4. Jesus Christ and God the Father

5. Your list may include the following:

- The Holy Spirit is with me constantly.

- The Holy Spirit will help me understand the Bible as I read it.

- The Holy Spirit will remind me of things I have learned.

- The Holy Spirit gives me the assurance of my salvation.

Week 1, Day 6

1. Personal Answers

Week 1, Day 7

1. Love others.

2. Obey His commandments.

3. Jesus died on the cross to save us.

Week Two

Week 2, Day 2

1. Personal Answers

Week 2, Day 3

1. Personal Answers

Week 2, Day 4

1. Personal Answers
2. Personal Answers

Week 2, Day 5

1. Personal Answers
2. Personal Answers
3. Personal Answers

Week 2, Day 6

1. God is pleased when I am broken over my sin and make a contrite confession of it from a heart that has been softened by conviction.

2. God does not take pleasure in the strength of man or military might; God takes pleasure in those who fear Him and hope in His mercy.

3. God does not take pleasure in our outward deeds but rather in our inward attitude towards Him. I must ask myself if I am doing justly to my fellow man, do I love mercy evidenced by how I interact with God and my fellow man, and do I walk humbly with my God.

4. I cannot please God if my mind is full of fleshly desires.

5. When the things of life get hard, I can please the Lord by remembering this life is only temporary, and He will give me grace to endure the hardness.

Week 2, Day 7

1. Eve did not believe God's warning about taking the forbidden fruit which resulted in the fall of the human race.

2. Sarah did not believe God's promise that she would bear a child, which resulted in a battle for the Promised Land which still rages today.

3. Rebekah did not believe God would keep His promise regarding her son, Jacob, and they both reaped the consequences of their deceitful actions.

4. Personal Answers

Week Three

Week 3, Day 2

1. Elisabeth and her husband, Zechariah, were obedient Christians. They were both elderly and had no children. The angel Gabriel came to Zechariah and told him Elisabeth was going to bear a Spirit-filled child who would prepare the way for Jesus. Later in the chapter we are told that Elisabeth was filled with the Holy Spirit and she praised God for the baby in Mary's womb.

2. Nothing

Week 3, Day 3

1. Priscilla was used along with her husband, Aquila, to teach Apollos the Word of God, and both had been willing to risk their lives for Paul and the gospel of Jesus Christ.

2. Nothing

Week 3, Day 4

1. Mary desired to sit at the feet of Jesus and commune with Him, which must come before our service for the Lord.
2. Nothing

Week 3, Day 5

1. She was someone who had been forgiven of much; therefore, she loved much.
2. Nothing

Week 3, Day 6

1. Deborah was both a prophetess and a judge, making her a well-respected leader. Barak was the commander of the army; however, he refused to go into battle without Deborah. She was willing to go, but made it clear the victory would not be in his honor, but rather God would use a woman to defeat Sisera.
2. Nothing
3. Jael was the brave heroine who was used of God to destroy an enemy of the Israelites.
4. Nothing

Week 3, Day 7

1. Tabitha was a woman who was full of good works and alms-deeds (giving to another out of a heart full of mercy or pity).
2. Nothing

3. Paul refers to Phebe as "our sister," which is a term of Christian endearment. He calls her a servant of the church and a succorer (one who is held in high esteem because she is a protector) of many.

4. Nothing

Week Four

Week 4, Day 2

1. Pride brings shame; lowliness brings wisdom.

2. Pride leads to destruction; God says humility is a better way.

3. Pride brings us down; humility leads to honor.

4. Pride brings us down, and will cause us to be humbled; humility brings a desire to serve others and will lead to being lifted up.

5. Pride is directly against the character of God; humility brings a likeness to Christ.

6. Pride brings resistance from God; humility brings grace from God.

Week 4, Day 3

1. God

2. She became a leper.

3. Aaron acknowledged their sin and asked for her healing, but Moses is the one who went to God on her behalf and secured a healing for her.

4. Personal answers

5. God promised Ahab He would not bring judgement during Ahab's lifetime because he had chosen to humble himself before the Lord.

Week 4, Day 4

1. Only four, but in the end, he also lost his wife.

2. Personal answers

3. Personal answers

4. Possible answers:

   • Perhaps they desired the same praise Barnabas received for his self-sacrifice.

   • Perhaps they did not want to be perceived as selfish for keeping any part of the proceeds of the sale.

   • Perhaps they simply wanted to be regarded as good people.

   • Perhaps they just wanted the attention for their gift.

5. Pride

Week 4, Day 5

1. Paul is concerned the young widows may become lazy and engage in foolish, vain babbling about the affairs of others, neglecting their own important matters.

2. The older women are commanded to teach the younger women to be serious about their responsibilities to love their husbands and children, to be discreet or temperate, to be chaste or pure, to be good homemakers, and to be obedient to their husbands.

3. Personal answers

4. Personal answers

Week 4, Day 6

1. Leah believed God gave her Reuben because He had seen her affliction. She hoped that in giving Jacob a son, she would also win his affection.

2. Leah believed God heard how Jacob treated her and gave her the blessing of another son.

3. After God blessed Leah with a third son, her hopes were high that Jacob would now feel an attachment to her.

4. Finally, after Leah's fourth son, she turns from her desire for Jacob's affection to simply praising the Lord for His goodness.

Week 4, Day 7

1. She clung to her and begged her not to insist that she return to her people and their gods. She proclaimed her desire to follow the God and people of Israel.

2. She offered to go and glean in the field of Elimelech's relative. Gleaning, following the reapers and picking up the scraps that remained, was practiced by those who were very poor.

3. Boaz saw her selfless service to Naomi in how hard she worked to provide for her. He also heard of the sacrifice she made in leaving her family and nation to care for her mother-in-law.

4. She instructed Ruth to wash herself and put on clean clothing.

5. Your list may include the following:

   • God gave Ruth a husband who would be able to care for her needs.

   • God gave Boaz and Ruth a son.

   • Naomi, who had lost both a husband and two sons, was able to have a part in caring for this new baby.

- This new baby's name was Obed, the father of Jesse, who was the father of David, in the direct lineage of Jesus Christ.

Week Five

Week 5, Day 2

1. He will help them.

2. God says that He will be a Father to them.

3. They should defend them.

4. Her nationality, that she was a Jew.

5. He kept checking on her.

6. She continued to obey Mordecai's request that she not let anyone know she was a Jew.

Week 5, Day 3

1. To go to the king and make a request that he intervene for the salvation of the Jews.

2. She was concerned for her life, should the king not receive her.

3. She asked that all of the Jews would fast for three days and three nights, along with her and her maidens, and then she would approach the king with a willingness to sacrifice her life for her people.

4. First of all, Haman's property and possessions were given to Esther which she, in turn, appointed Mordecai to oversee on her behalf. The king then promoted Mordecai to the same position Haman had held. Because the law forbade the king from reversing his original edict, new letters were written

which essentially nullified the first by allowing the Jews to defend themselves and to take the possessions of the enemies they defeated. The Jews gained so much respect from the people that many chose to become Jews.

Week 5, Day 4

1. The Bible says he was churlish (hardhearted or obstinate) and evil. The Bible also tells us he was a man of prosperity.

2. He rudely refused to help them.

3. Abigail very quickly gathered provisions for David and his men and then humbly sought his forgiveness. She also used wisdom to caution David in his quest for vengeance.

4. He removed the man who had caused her much pain and gave her a place of honor as the king's wife.

Week 5, Day 5

1. Author's suggestions

2. Author's suggestions

3. Author's suggestions

Week 5, Day 6

1. The stories from the Old Testament serve as examples and, hopefully, deterrents to guide us away from sin and lead us toward spiritual victory.

2. The next generation will forget how God intervened for their forefathers and will suffer the consequences of failing to acknowledge His work in their lives.

3. Personal answers

<u>Week 5, Day 7</u>

1. If I am to have the fear of the Lord, I must hate the sins that will make me unwilling to hear His instructions.

2. If I am to have the fear of the Lord, I must be willing to humble myself to reproof and instruction.

3. Living with the fear of the Lord brings satisfaction, and although evil may be meant toward us, we can trust in God's Word and believe that He will use it for good.

4. When we live in the fear of the Lord, we can trust in His protection.

5. I will not find wisdom, nor understanding, apart from the fear of the Lord.

Week Six

<u>Week 6, Day 2</u>

1. I am wise when I hate the things God hates.

2. I am wise when I have a desire to be instructed.

3. I am wise when I both fear and depart from sinful ways.

4. I am wise when I am willing to accept correction.

5. I am wise when I have a desire to tell others the gospel message.

6. I am wise when I have a desire to both hear and obey God's commandments.

7. I am wise when I choose not to harbor bitterness, envying, and strife in my heart.

Week 6, Day 3

1. I am to judge them by God's truths and then bring them under submission to those truths.

2. The truth of the Word of God.

3. Possible answers:

   - I should first bring my cares to God in prayer remembering to thank Him.

   - I should think or meditate upon the qualities that are exemplified in the life of Christ: truth, or reality based upon the truths of God's Word, honesty, justness, purity, things that are lovely or pleasing, things of good report, things that are virtuous, things that are praiseworthy.

4. He wants me to rule over it.

5. I can expect to experience gladness, joy, happiness, and peace.

Week 6, Day 4

1. I must forgive if I hope to be forgiven. I must show mercy if I desire to find mercy with God.

2. I must forgive as often as I desire God to forgive me for my repetitive sins.

Week 6, Day 5

1. It will help motivate me to keep myself pure.

2. Father, please show me truth in your Word and convict me of any areas in my heart, or thoughts that are not pleasing to you.

3. He humbly recognized his need for mercy.

4. He acknowledged his sin and the fact that it was first and foremost against God.

5. Possible answers:

- He desired to have his joy back.

- He desired for God not to view him as he really is.

- He desired God to do a work of restoration in giving him a new, clean heart and a new spirit.

- He desired God's fellowship.

- He desired to be restored to the former relationship he had with God.

- He desired for God to uphold him, and to keep him from falling by the power of His Spirit.

- He desired to be used of God once again.

- He desired to praise Him for he knew God does not desire a show of sacrifice when we sin, but rather a quiet surrendering of the heart and a personal contrition and confession of sin.

Week 6, Day 6

1. The Bible says they are wise.

2. Answers may include the following:

- Paul states his choice to be a servant of Christ to help win the lost.

- Paul states he is willing to lay aside his Christian liberties in order to win the lost.

- Paul is willing to do more than the law required, to live in such a way that he could win the lost.

3. Win the lost, baptize them, and then teach them what I have taught you.

Week 6, Day 7

1. Personal answers

About the Author

Robin has served in full-time ministry with her husband, Dan, for more than forty years and holds a Bachelor of Science degree in education. She is a Sunday school teacher, a ladies' conference speaker, a personal mentor, and has had many articles published in a Christian ladies' magazine. Sensing the increasing needs of women in the 21st century, she sought further training from several biblical counseling ministries and has earned certifications from two of them.

While these things would be considered Robin's "credentials," she would prefer to simply be known as a wife, mother of four, and grandmother of twelve. She has a great love for her Colorado mountains and enjoys the lessons God gives through His book of nature. She would be quick to tell you that she is not a Bible scholar, but she does love the insight given by studying words from their Greek and Hebrew meanings. It is her desire to rightly divide the Word of Truth and bring a new perspective to the importance we, as women, place upon our physical appearance. The philosophy of the world in which we live has had a great influence upon our thinking about physical beauty. May you find within these pages a transformation by renewing your mind and trusting God's will in His creation of you. *"And be not conformed to this world: but be ye transformed by the renewing of your mind, that ye may prove what is that good, and acceptable, and perfect, will of God"* (Rom. 12:2).

CPSIA information can be obtained
at www.ICGtesting.com
Printed in the USA
JSHW020017200920
7927JS00002B/4